BEING LIKE JESUS:
100 DAYS TO MORE SUCCESS, SATISFACTION, AND LIVING ON PURPOSE

by
DR. CURTIS ALEXANDER

Most Leadership Books products are available at special quantity discounts for bulk purchases for sales promotions, premiums, fund-raising and educational needs. For details visit our website at www.leadershipbooks.com

Being Like Jesus: 100 Days to More Success, Satisfaction and Living on Purpose

Published by Leadership Books *or*
Published by Pharresia, an imprint of Leadership Books.
Las Vegas, Nevada & New York, NY

This book or parts thereof may not be reproduced in any form, stored in a retrieval system, or transmitted in any form by any means – electronic, mechanical, photocopy, recording, or otherwise- without prior written permission of the publisher, except as provided by United States of America copyright law. Permission may be granted upon request.

Copyright 2024 by Dr. Curtis Alexander

All rights reserved.

Hardcover: 978-1-951648-32-9
Paperback: 978-1-951648-35-0
eBook: 978-1-951648-39-8

Unless otherwise noted, all Scripture readings are from The Holy Bible, New International Version® NIV®. Copyright © 1973, 1978, 1984, 2011 by Biblica Inc.® Used by permission of Biblica, Inc.® All rights reserved worldwide.
New American Standard Bible® NASB® Copyright © 1960, 1971, 1977, 1995, 2020 by The Lockman Foundation A Corporation Not for Profit La Habra, CA All Rights Reserved www.lockman.org
Holy Bible, New Living Translation, copyright © 1996, 2004, 2015 by Tyndale House Foundation. All Rights Reserved. Used by permission of Tyndale House Publishers, Carol Stream, Illinois 60188. All rights reserved.
While the author has made every effort to provide accurate internet addresses at the time of publication, neither the publisher nor the author assumes any responsibility for errors or for changes that occur after publication. Further, the publisher does not have any control over and does not assume any responsibility for the author or third-party website or their content.

To contact Dr. Alexander, send emails to: ckalex1402@gmail.com

Dedication

This book is dedicated to a few people who are closest to my heart.

First, my wife of many years, Kathy, has listened to so many ideas and pieces of writing, she is a saint for putting up with me. Also I dedicate BEING LIKE JESUS to my kids who provided so much insight and so many examples that have proven useful in my decades of speaking to audiences and the books that have come from our shared experiences.

Finally, I dedicate this book to my mentor and Editor–in–Chief of *Missionary Church TODAY magazine, Dr. Tom Murphy. You have inspired me and showed me how to live a life of service to God.*

I love you all.

Curtis Alexander, Palmetto, FL, July, 2024

TABLE OF CONTENTS

Dedication iii

Prologue: Leaving a Legacy vii

Introduction: How to reach the goal of Being Like Jesus ix

What Would Jesus Think? (Day 1 – 12) 1

What is God Like? (Day 13–25) 37

God of Wonders, Beyond our Galaxy (Day 26–37) 77

Life's Five Love Values (Day 38–52) 111

God's Glory and Pleasure (Day 53–64) 155

Honest to Goodness (Day 65–73) 185

Living with Follow-Through (Day 74–87) 211

This Means War! (Day 88–100) 253

Epilogue: A life of ordered priorities 291

PREFACE/PROLOGUE
Prologue: Leaving a Legacy

My wife Kathy and I are driven to leave a godly heritage for future generations. When I first mentioned writing this book, she said, "Think of how it could impact our kids and grandkids, even after we're gone."

My second motivation for writing *Being Like Jesus* is that people who do not even know us might benefit from our lifetime of experiences, both our failures and our successes.

My personal timeline stretches from a party-line, crank-it telephone in the early 1960s, to today's worldwide descent into a much-debated moral and ethical abyss. I've learned good and plenty (and almost as much as I have forgotten) in my time as college professor, seminary dean, editor, musician, Christian broadcaster, and pastor. Other life experiences include being in the 101st Airborne, factory work, sales, and construction. And like many, I also painted houses during college summer breaks, many, many years ago.

Secretly, I will admit my life has not been so interesting that I would encourage anyone to read a book about it. I wouldn't want to read that book either.

But *Being Like Jesus* isn't about me. It's about Jesus—and you. As you read it, think about how He can radically transform you into a more faithful, enthusiastic, and effective follower who shines the Light of the World into the dark corners of so many lives.

One song that captures the sense of adventure involved in Being Like Jesus is a Steven Curtis Chapman tune. In it, he sings that blazing a trail through God's amazing grace is a life like no other. Click on the link below to get the full benefit of this remarkable song.

(Visit YouTube.com to watch Steven Curtis Chapman,"The Great Adventure")

INTRODUCTION

How to Reach the Lofty Goal of Being Like Jesus

Everyone grows up to be like someone. It may mean inheriting a large nose from Dad or Mom, a duck–like waddle from your family's genetics or bone structure (I've been fingered for that one), or a shrill, irritating cackle that runs in the family.

Maybe it applies to our personality, temperament, and how we navigate our way through life's challenges. Psychologists say that during our teen years, many examine and weigh the values and principles we've learned from parents and others. During this process, we decide which beliefs to embrace as our own, and which to discard. Often our ways can be traced back to someone else. We grow up to be like good old so–and–so.

This reflection of others in our lives also has a spiritual component. Jesus told the bullies tormenting Him, "You belong to your father, the devil, and you want to carry out your father's desires. He was a murderer from the beginning, not holding to the truth, for there is no truth in him. When he lies, he speaks his native language, for he is a liar and the father of lies" (John 8:44). In other words, Jesus was telling them they bore a striking resemblance to the devil. Ouch!

It's also possible to end up reminding others of your Savior, Jesus. Hence, the title of this book, *Being Like Jesus!*

> **All of us turn out being like someone else. Why not set out on the path to become like Jesus? This book shows the way to a rewarding life of success, satisfaction, and living on purpose.**

While we cannot influence things like a big nose, a cackle, or a walk at which others snicker, we do have wide latitude to think, speak, and act in our lives. At one horrible extreme, we can choose to imitate the father of lies who also happens to be a murderer. At the other extreme we can set out to pattern our mental/emotional, spiritual, and social aspects of life after Jesus.

This book is intended to help you become more like Jesus. There can be no possible reason to choose a Satan–likeness over being like Jesus. But millions upon millions (maybe billions) do just that.

I'm convinced that reading *Being Like Jesus* day after day will support the wannabe Jesus follower to achieve this lofty and noble goal. Along the way I believe it will enhance success, satisfaction, and a life of purpose to a degree unattainable any other way.

Consider this your personal invitation to shape your life in the pattern of the One who laid aside the unfathomable riches of heaven and took up the divinely distasteful life of a human being on this fallen planet. Finally He made the ultimate sacrifice for you and me, laying down His life, so we can enjoy the resources of His greatest plans and goals for us.

Being Like Jesus is structured into 100 brief essays. You can read one in the time it takes to drink your first cup of morning joe. These daily essays are designed to set the tone for your day. You can read from Day 1 through to Day 100, or choose a chapter that interests you. Or, just jump around from one essay to another. Go ahead and journal in the Interact sections, if you enjoy that sort of thing. You'll find that it will add to the value you get from this book.

When using the "Interact" journal sections, feel free to respond however you like. Elaborating on one or two items may be best for you. Also, you may enjoy discussing various issues verbally with someone else who is a budding Jesus follower. Journaling along with someone else who is reading *Being Like Jesus* can also be very meaningful. If you are not a journaling type, just skip over the Interact sections. I believe you'll still find the book powerfully insightful, as well as interesting and useful.

Any reader who pursues these principles with some diligence will begin to think, speak, and act more like Jesus. And there you have it, a reliable recipe for success, satisfaction, and living on purpose.

Ahoy, Mate. Celebrate the voyage and enjoy the cruise!

—Dr. Curtis Alexander, Hancock, Michigan, September 2023

1
WHAT WOULD JESUS THINK?

(Days 1–12)
To enrich your experience in Chapter One, go to www.YouTube.com and watch Word of God Speak, "MercyMe"

DAY 1
SECULAR VERSUS CHRISTIAN

> "Therefore, I urge you, brothers and sisters, in view of God's mercy, to offer your bodies as a living sacrifice, holy and pleasing to God— this is your true and proper worship.² Do not conform to the pattern of this world, but be transformed by the renewing of your mind. Then you will be able to test and approve what God's will is—his good, pleasing and perfect will."—Romans 12:1–2

WORLDVIEW is how we look at and fit into the world around us. Everyone has a worldview, even if you've never thought about it.

There are two prominent worldviews in today's culture: secular life and Christian life. Patrick Morley in *The Man in the Mirror* writes that people who identify as Christians also divide into two camps, *biblical* Christians and *secular* Christians.

Secular means unspiritual, up to and including anti–Christian thinking. Some use the words 'secular,' 'worldly,' and 'the flesh' interchangeably. Statistics show that with social issues like divorce, living together before marriage, abortion, homosexuality, and others, there's little visible difference between people who call themselves Christians and the secular society around us. Christians may or may not have a biblical worldview shaped by what the Bible teaches.

In *Think Like Jesus,* George Barna admits that his own Christian life was "a haphazard series of disjointed choices only marginally and inconsistently influenced by my faith." But again, it is the *biblical* at war with the *secular*. How will people decide what to think, say and do when the heat is on?

"A biblical worldview is *thinking like Jesus*. It is a way of making our faith practical to every situation we face each day." A biblical worldview interfaces with the world so that we *act* like Jesus in the world 24/7 because we *think* like Jesus.

You can make the right decisions, even when the future is on the line. If you think like Jesus, you can succeed in your decision making. Those Jesus–thoughts will become Jesus–words and Jesus–actions. We can be transformed into people who think, speak, and act like God (Ephesians 5:1). He will reward anyone who pursues His transformation for their lives. Thinking like Jesus is not like a shirt you wear, take off, and throw in the laundry. It's a constant way of life.

Someone said, "God loves you just the way you are. But He loves you too much to leave you just the way you are."

> Secular Christians and purely secular people don't ask, "What would Jesus do in this situation?" They ask, "What decision is most likely to get me what I want?"

WHAT'S THE POINT?: *Are you truly biblical in your decision making, or is the secular worldview your default choice? Until you can say, "I want to think, speak, and act like Jesus," God's transformation in your life is merely a pipe dream.*

PRAYER: *Jesus, please reveal to me the way I look at the world—my 'worldview.' Am I a secular Christian? If so, help me develop a biblical worldview that reflects Your view of this fallen world, with the goal of redeeming it. Success in life depends on it. Amen!*

INTERACT:

How has God's will in your life been good, pleasing, and perfect?

_____
_____
_____
_____
_____

God's transformation can happen in my life when I

_____
_____
_____
_____
_____

What makes you believe your worldview is biblical?

_____
_____
_____
_____
_____

Suppose your mind is a computer on which you can make new files, and delete old files. To be more like Jesus, which files do you want to add, and which would you delete?

_____

_____

_____

_____

_____

DAY 2
LUST FOR PLAYTHINGS, PLEASURES AND PRIDE

> "For everything in the world—the lust of the flesh, the lust of the eyes, and the pride of life—comes not from the Father but from the world." —1 John 2:16

It is so easy (convenient, comfortable, rational) to conform to the behavior and customs of this world. It is the default option for decision-making and behavior for all who want their way more than they want Jesus's way.

Sinful cravings are the first behaviors identified in 1 John 2:16. Secular thinkers evaluate things and make decisions that will gratify their selfish passions and gain more material goods, even at the cost of meaningful family and friend relationships. This is the worship of self and the things we want. Unfortunately, it's the custom of this world, as Paul wrote in Romans 12:2, to crave something that will bankrupt your soul.

And then there's *physical lust and pleasure.* The lust for physical pleasure is a specific behavior of this world. It is one of the devil's favorites. This worldview evaluates relationships based on how much selfish pleasure they can give you. It devalues people, demeans your inclination to godliness, and results in failure, frustration, and emptiness.

Boasting about what we have, and what we've done, *and self-centered pride* makes up the third behavior—typical of those who value the things of the world more than God. The world's custom is to brag about what you have. That's one of the reasons people acquire ever more stuff—for the bragging rights. Others live to brag about what they have done, where they have gone, and the people they know.

Both kinds of bragging fulfill the secular worldview that feeds personal pride at the expense of positive relationships with self, others, and especially with God.

> Sinful cravings combined with physical lust lead us to love things and use people, when we should love people and use things.

WHAT'S THE POINT?: *When we conform to the behavior and customs of the world around us, we devalue human beings; we lust for pleasure and are filled with egocentric pride. Only a Christ-centered worldview can free us from this self-inflicted bondage.*

PRAYER: *God, please show me the materialism, lust for pleasure, and pride that may be crippling my relationships and shriveling my soul. Amen!*

INTERACT: What did the apostle John mean by the "world" in today's verse?

_____
_____
_____
_____

Describe a time you stood up for your biblical viewpoint in the face of secular pressure (and/or a time you caved).

_____
_____
_____
_____

WHAT WOULD JESUS THINK?

How would people who know you finish the statement, "I know you think like Jesus because..." (Hint: See Day 10)

_____

_____

_____

_____

_____

DAY 3
FROM WORM TO WONDER

> "All Scripture is God-breathed and is useful for teaching, rebuking, correcting and training in righteousness,[17] so that the servant of God may be thoroughly equipped for every good work."
> —2 Timothy 3:16–17

Paul urged the Romans, "Let God transform you." In contrast to being shaped by the world's pattern, he encouraged his readers to be transformed into Christ followers. How does this happen? By learning to think like Jesus. Paul called it the renewing of your mind. The result of being transformed is that you will understand God's good, pleasing, and perfect will for your life. The original New Testament language uses the word *metamorphosis* (Romans 12:2).

When our kids were small, we rented a house near the Bible College I attended. One morning, coming down the porch steps, I noticed a cocoon in the forsythia bush. Throughout the day, we watched the metamorphosis of a caterpillar. The transformation from ugly worm to beautiful butterfly almost took my breath away.

One definition of metamorphosis is "a profound change in form from one stage to the next in the life history of an organism." That's biology. But it is also about transforming our hearts. It's what God wants to do for the Christian.

The first building block for being like Jesus is His *Foundation*—the Word of God. Some preachers try to paint this transformation as fast and painless. They suggest, "To be successful, just do this… It's easy; there's nothing to it!" But the truly Christlike life takes effort and, yes, time. Learning about how Jesus thinks by learning the Bible is a noble yet demanding, time-consuming endeavor. There is no way to reduce the process of being like Jesus to a quick, easy formula. That's why Paul told Timothy to be a "worker" (2 Timothy 2:15).

WHAT'S THE POINT?: *You can never become like Jesus without paying careful attention to what the Bible teaches. It takes effort and dedication, but its reward is an amazing metamorphosis from an ugly worm into a beautiful creation of God that soars into the wild blue yonder!*

> "Christ-likeness is your eventual destination, but your journey will last a lifetime."
> —Rick Warren

PRAYER: *Precious Lord, I'm really interested in the transformation that comes from learning and obeying Your Word. Please start the process in me. Amen!*

INTERACT: What's involved in "being transformed into God's image" (2 Corinthians 3:18)?

_____

_____

_____

_____

_____

If I'm being transformed into Jesus's image, these things will have to change in my life:

_____

_____

_____

_____

_____

The most powerful influence on me for decision making is

To manage the time it will take to gain proficiency in the Bible, I will need to

DAY 4

SPIRITUAL INSUBORDINATION

> "So I say, walk by the Spirit, and you will not gratify the desires of the flesh.[17] For the flesh desires what is contrary to the Spirit, and the Spirit what is contrary to the flesh. They are in conflict with each other, so that you are not to do whatever you want."
> —Galatians 5:16–17

The devil tells us that any statement with the word *spiritual* is not actually about reality. You know, spirituality is just a fuzzy idea floating around out there like milkweed silk or air pollution. This is a lie. Spiritual insubordination is real. It affects everything in life, from relationships to success or failure to the tragedy of toe fungus (OK, maybe not that).

First, the Jesus follower is building on the Bible, the Foundation upon which Jesus established His earthly life. Once you get the right fundamentals, you can focus on developing the same overall goal in life that Jesus had. Focus on knowing and doing God's good, pleasing, and perfect will.

You will only be like Jesus and have His divine success once you willingly submit your direction in life to Him.

The fact is that we want our own way, not God's. This is at the core of most human unhappiness, frustration, and suffering. The rebellious life of a secular thinker is saturated with the refusal to let God lead where He wants you to go.

If you push Jesus off and seize your life's throne, He will let you: He is a Gentleman, and will give you your own way. But He never blesses selfishness. Not a good formula for success, satisfaction, or living on purpose.

Transforming from world–thinking to Jesus–thinking takes a step of faith. It means surrendering control, trusting God to do what's best for you; He looks out for your interests in a way you cannot do for yourself. Embrace God's way instead of your own. There's only room for one person on life's throne, and God will not share it with anyone.

> **We're prone to insubordination, refusing God His rightful place at the leading edge of life.**

WHAT'S THE POINT?: *If you don't willingly follow God's path for you, then you're on your own. Good luck managing your life, a task more complicated than brain surgery, rocket science, or understanding the opposite sex.*

PRAYER: *Father God, remind me of my past rebellious insubordination. Please show me the path of surrendering to, and obeying, You. Then I can experience Your brand of true success in my life. Amen!*

INTERACT: In what ways has the conflict between "the flesh" and the Spirit made your life more difficult?

_____
_____
_____
_____
_____

One example of choosing my own way over God's way is:

_____
_____
_____
_____
_____

I would have more success and fulfillment in my life if I surrendered to God in this way:

_____

_____

_____

_____

_____

DAY 5

KEEP YOUR FILTER CLEAN

> "If any of you lacks wisdom, you should ask God, who gives generously to all without finding fault, and it will be given to you."
> —James 1:5

Besides Jesus's Foundation (God's Word) and His Focus or goal (God's will), we need His Filter (God's wisdom). Whenever Jesus thought about circumstances or decisions He had to make, He applied godly wisdom (instead of earthly intellectualism) to the problem He faced. If an idea couldn't get through the filter of God's wisdom, Jesus knew it was from the secular world and not from His Father. This godly wisdom uncovers the source of the voice whispering in your ear. Is it God or is it the evil one?

Jesus steadfastly refused to act in any way that didn't pass the test of God's wisdom, "Would God approve of this thought, word, or action?" and, "Would Father God say this, or does it sound more like what the devil would say?" If Jesus could not see God approving a particular decision, He would not do it.

So how do you get true godly wisdom to filter your decisions? Ask God for wisdom (James 1:5), and He promises to give it to you. But, of course, it doesn't happen instantly. Learn what the Bible teaches and how Jesus thought, spoke, and acted. Examine yourself to see where your selfishness bursts through the surface like a fish after a worm. God's wisdom is only available to those who are willing to work for it, like panning for gold.

Wanting your own way doesn't end when you reach adulthood. Finding and following God's will instead of your own is a lifelong process because selfish desire is a lifelong problem.

If you ignore or reject the biblical worldview, will God still give you His wisdom? Of course not. Why would He? Many people say, "Lord, tell me Your will for this decision, then I will decide whether to follow You or my own path." God never plays that game. He knows your heart, so it doesn't work to pretend you will follow His lead—He already knows.

WHAT'S THE POINT?: *Being like Jesus means applying God's wisdom to your decisions—to honestly answer the question, "What does godly wisdom tell me?" and then follow it.*

PRAYER: *Dear Lord Jesus, please give me Your filter, the precious gift of godly wisdom. Then help me apply it to my decisions in life. Amen!*

> **Jesus steered clear of 'earthly wisdom' because He wanted to please God, not Himself or those around Him.**

INTERACT: How do you feel about knowing God is not a fault finder?

_____
_____
_____
_____

A time I used God's wisdom to filter a decision was

_____
_____
_____
_____

A time my selfish desires kept me from following God's will was___

_____

_____

_____

_____

_____

Describe one time you had the attitude, "God, show me Your will, and I'll decide if I want to follow it."

_____

_____

_____

_____

_____

DAY 6
4F: FOUNDATION, FOCUS, FILTER, FAITH

> "For I am not ashamed of the gospel, because it is the power of God that brings salvation to everyone who believes: first to the Jew, then to the Gentile.[17] For in the gospel the righteousness of God is revealed—a righteousness that is by faith from first to last, just as it is written: 'The righteous will live by faith.'"
> **—Romans 1:16–17**

Jesus was 4F, and I don't mean physically unfit for military service! Today we bring Days 3 through 6 together. You can't have one without the others.

Webster defines *Faith* as a firm belief in something for which there is no empirical proof. Synonyms include trust, loyalty, fidelity, belief, allegiance, and devotion. Jesus's faith caused Him to act on His godly beliefs. He didn't just think or say it. His actions were grounded in what He believed. If you trust God to do what He says, in Scripture, it means you have genuine faith in Him. You believe what He has said, trust His promises, have confidence in Him and are committed to follow and obey Christ.

The result of Jesus's transformation of your life is not just some fuzzy, foggy otherworldly, squishy, ambiguous feeling. The result of faith is a reality of success, satisfaction, and purpose. It offers a full, overflowing, rewarding life.

I admit, Jesus had a heavenly matrix for His faith. He was there when the divine Trinity said, "Let's create the heavens and the earth and make humankind in Our own image." Further, Jesus was the divine Agent of all creation: "… in Him all things were created" (Colossians 1:16).

Once Jesus confirmed that His thoughts lined up with His Father's thoughts, He was free to act according to His *Faith* that had its *Foundation* in Scripture, was *Focused* on the goal of doing God's will and always *Filtered* through godly wisdom.

Unlike Jesus, we were not there when God created the universe. We didn't see firsthand Jesus's miracles: healing the sick, controlling nature, feeding the hungry, or raising the dead. And yet, He calls us to emulate His faith, belief, and trust. In that way we complete the circuit of a true Christian worldview, becoming more and more like Jesus. Our transformation can proceed without delay when we grow into a trusting, devoted, submissive person of faith, being like Jesus.

You may know people who declare that they live by faith, but do they? Their actions may not match up with what they say. They pay lip service to beliefs they don't actually hold. Maybe they think it would help them get their way, or they want to impress others. Perhaps they don't want to disappoint someone else by being honest about their true beliefs. Possibly, they're closet secular thinkers living around people who prize biblical values. Whatever their reason for being dishonest about what they believe, their lives are inconsistent. It's a very unpleasant way to live.

If you choose to live out your faith in practical ways, only God knows how exciting, successful, and satisfying your life will be. In fact, you could never engineer a life half as wonderful by using secular thinking.

> **When our thoughts, words, and actions are consistent with what we really believe (our faith), the sky's the limit.**

WHAT'S THE POINT?: *When you constantly think, speak, and act like Jesus, demonstrating His Fundamentals, Focus, Filter and Faith, God's version of success will become your own.*

PRAYER: *Heavenly Father, please help me be consistent in thought, word and action. Then I will emulate my Savior, Jesus Christ. Amen!*

INTERACT: What would it be worth to "have a righteousness that is by faith from first to last"?

_____

_____

_____

_____

Martin Luther struggled with hyper–legalism until he read Romans 1:16–17. How could today's Scripture passage revolutionize *your* life?

_____

_____

_____

_____

One time that my actions betrayed my lip service to my beliefs was

_____

_____

_____

_____

When Jesus transforms your life most effectively, what will be different about you?

_____

_____

_____

_____

_____

These people (names, please) will be supportive when God's transformation is changing me from the inside out:

_____

_____

_____

_____

DAY 7
FILING FOR MORAL BANKRUPTCY

> "I will say to myself, 'You have plenty of grain laid up for many years. Take life easy; eat, drink and be merry.'"[20] "But God said to him, 'You fool! This very night your life will be demanded from you. Then who will get what you have prepared for yourself?'[21] "This is how it will be with whoever stores up things for themselves but is not rich toward God."
> —Luke 12:19–21

Changing your thinking sounds easy, but experience proves it's harder than it seems. The longer you have thought the way the world does, the more difficult it will be to change. Becoming a Jesus thinker and follower can be challenging, demanding work. There are plenty of failures, backtracking, and Mulligan do–overs. Some fixing of past mistakes is needed. But changing your thought patterns can be very rewarding.

Bankrupt secular thinking is permeated by two values, Francis Shaeffer said in his classic book, *How Should We Then Live?* The first is *the quest for personal peace—to be left alone.* Secular thinkers don't want to be bothered by other people's problems and troubles. This is the desire to live with the smallest possibility of being personally disturbed.

Second is the gold standard of secular thinking, *affluence.* Overwhelming, ever–increasing prosperity is the human drive to acquire material stuff, leisure, and pleasure. A majority of secular thinkers' decisions are based on whether or not the decision will contribute to their own personal space and owning ever more possessions and pleasure.

A third impoverished value is the *comfort* of religion without the demands of commitment, sacrifice, or service to anyone but themselves.

I constantly wrestle against letting this world's secular worldview dominate my decisions and my way of thinking. That may not impact you much, but all three of these hit me below the belt! It's a recipe for moral bankruptcy:

1. Leave me alone.
2. Get as much money and stuff as I can.
3. Give me a religion that makes no demands on me.

Many of us have to learn this lesson over and over. Greed, personal comfort, and easy religion all seem inviting, but caring about people is better than prizing personal comfort and possessions. It's possible to change how you think. Thinking like Jesus is best.

> Moral bankruptcy: 1) Greed is good; 2) Don't bother me; and; 3) Give me religion that costs me nothing.

WHAT'S THE POINT?: *There's irony that serving yourself while excluding others is a most unsatisfying way to live. Yet, the paradox is, serving others is the best way to find success, satisfaction, and a life of godly purpose.*

PRAYER: *Lord God, please draw me to those who need my help. Only when I focus outwardly will I have satisfaction inwardly. Amen!*

INTERACT: As a Jesus thinker, do I need a do-over in this circumstance?

I have shown moral/ethical weakness in at least one of these areas. God, help me to

_____

_____

_____

_____

_____

A practical sign that I prefer my religion easy and comfortable is

_____
_____
_____
_____
_____

- Use this scale to measure how rich you are toward God.

0	1	2	3	4	5	6	7	8	9	10
Me, myself, my treasures				Making ends meet				God is my wealth manager		

DAY 8

WHY THINK LIKE JESUS?

> "'For I know the plans I have for you,' declares the LORD, 'plans to prosper you and not to harm you, plans to give you hope and a future.'" —Jeremiah 29:11

> "The person with the Spirit makes judgments about all things, but such a person is not subject to merely human judgments,"[16] for, "Who has known the mind of the Lord so as to instruct him? But we have the mind of Christ."
> —1 Corinthians 2:15–16

In sales training, they teach you to describe and explain the *benefits* of what you're selling, not just its *features*; "Here's why it is so great to own this widget I am selling." If you only talk about features, the potential buyer may miss why owning your product or service is so wonderful.

It is vitally important to understand the benefits of being a Jesus thinker. There are as many perks to thinking like Jesus as there are individuals on Earth. Here are four universal perks; you may want to add them to your list.

There's increased meaning and enjoyment in life. When you think like Jesus and become transformed by God, life has a new sense of meaning and worth it never had before. You can enjoy and value life because of your biblical worldview in myriad ways no secular thinker can.

Confusion becomes order. Chaos reigns in your earthly thinking if your beliefs about right and wrong, good and bad, useful and useless, are shaped by the world around you instead of God's word. When you begin to think like Jesus, your life, even your troubles, begin to make sense. When you trust Jesus through trying or tragic circumstances, you have hope for the future, even when those around you are caving in to hopeless despair.

You gain a sense of hope and anticipation, when you think like Jesus. Even if it seems that the world rejects your Christian values, you can see that God still honors and blesses people who think like Jesus. You're safe in His hands, no matter what threatens to harm you.

Thinking like Jesus benefits you because *you can find God's plan for your life.* He has an exciting path for you to follow. Nothing in this world gives the secular thinker that assurance.

WHAT'S THE POINT?: *Life is tough enough. So, why make it impossible by following anyone but Jesus? He has your best interests at heart, and has everything under control.*

> "The scripture is God's plan on how we are to live our lives here, and what we are to do to have eternal life."
> —Deborah Norville

PRAYER: *Dear Lord Jesus, thank You for the wonderful benefits of thinking like You. Even when I don't understand why things happen, I trust You to fulfill Your plan for me and to make my life meaningful and satisfying. Amen!*

INTERACT: Though Jeremiah 29:11 articulated God's promise to the Jews in exile, how does it apply to you today?

_____

_____

_____

_____

God has blessed me for thinking like Jesus in this way

_____

_____

_____

How has being more like Jesus given you hope in a dark time?

List at least a dozen perks to thinking like Jesus:

DAY 9
YOU'RE IN GOOD HANDS, BEING LIKE JESUS

> "Do not be anxious about anything, but in every situation, by prayer and petition, with thanksgiving, present your requests to God.[7] And the peace of God, which transcends all understanding, will guard your hearts and your minds in Christ Jesus."
> —Philippians 4:6–7

Dietrich Bonhoeffer was an anti–Nazi pastor executed mere days before liberation. Bonhoeffer was accused of being involved in a plot against Hitler's life. He wrote the classic book, *The Cost of Discipleship*, which explores what being like Jesus might cost the modern disciple.

The cost of being like Jesus may seem high, but not following Him costs even more. In this life, not following Jesus will cost you guilt, fear, anger, and frustration. Worse, it will cost eternal life. Following Jesus through life is the best decision you could ever make. Being like Jesus offers a wealth of benefits.

One of the greatest benefits is fulfilling relationships. Aristotle described three levels of friendship: personal usefulness (what you get out of it), selfish pleasure, and mutual benefit. Two of these levels are self–centered. But thinking like Jesus creates mutually beneficial relationships, where everyone profits. If a marriage relationship is between two self–centered people who don't care about pleasing the other, it cannot profit either of them. It's also unlikely to last.

More meaningful work is another advantage. Thinking like Jesus integrates your faith into every area of life, including vocation. It gives new purpose, satisfaction and success to your labor. Being like Jesus makes you a better coworker, a more valuable employee, or a more effective boss.

A biblical worldview enhances your ability to cope with life's high and low points. You can trust that Jesus knows what's best for you, even when you don't understand what He's doing. He will help you deal with any problem you may face, even tragedy. He can lovingly shape the entire scope of your life if you'll surrender to Him.

Those who think like Jesus know what is truly important and what is not. They are not held captive by the world's corrupted ideas of value and worth. They can survive life's troubles as temporary obstacles to eternal joy and peace.

Bearing the name 'Christian' implies that you pattern your life after Jesus. No wonder Jesus too often gets a bad reputation in the world, when secular– thinking Christians are the foremost visible evidence of what Jesus is like. When you think like the world, you will speak and act like the world. Who would be attracted to Jesus by that?

> **Jesus thinkers are not corrupted by what the world says is true or important. They see the benefits of Being Like Jesus!**

WHAT'S THE POINT?: *Benefits for the Jesus follower keep on accumulating. Why would anyone choose the stress, frustration, and defeat that result from thinking like the failed, bankrupt world around them?*

PRAYER: *Heavenly Father, please help me show the people around me that being like Jesus is a life of success, satisfaction, and godly purpose. May others be attracted to You by my life. Amen!*

INTERACT: What has your discipleship already cost you?

_____

_____

_____

_____

As you grow more like Jesus, what personal benefits do you expect to reap?

_____
_____
_____
_____

Write about one fulfilling relationship that has blessed you because you think like Jesus.

_____
_____
_____
_____

How has your hope for the future changed as you have grown closer to Jesus?

_____
_____
_____
_____

One difficulty in life that I overcame through following Jesus was

_____
_____
_____
_____

DAY 10

SIGNS OF A JESUS THINKER

> "In your relationships with one another, have the same mindset as Christ Jesus: ⁶Who, being in very nature God, did not consider equality with God something to be used to his own advantage; ⁷rather, he made himself nothing by taking the very nature of a servant, being made in human likeness. ⁸And being found in appearance as a man, he humbled himself by becoming obedient to death—
> even death on a cross!"
> —Philippians 2:5–8

While most Jesus thinkers share common ground in many things, there is always room for respectful disagreement in some beliefs. But there are also tenets of the Faith that every Jesus thinker with a biblical worldview embraces.

Comedian Jeff Foxworthy might put it this way, *"You know you're a Jesus thinker if..."*

- *you acknowledge the supernatural.* Jesus Christ is God in the flesh. You know that if God is who He says He is in the Bible, miracles are no problem for Him. If He created the universe by the word of His mouth, healing a sick person or even resurrecting the dead is easy. It doesn't even raise a sweat.
- *you affirm the reality of absolute truth.* It's not simply relative to the circumstances or times. Truth is not whatever you want to believe; it is what God wants you to believe.
- *you have an all–inclusive view of self and service*—your Christianity is not just a little part of you. It's who you are. It saturates everything you do. Serving God and blessing others is the reason for life.

You are here to make a difference in a world crushed by evil and confused by the lies of the devil.

- *you are aware of evil in the world.* You acknowledge the fall of humanity into sin and the ongoing struggle against evil in your personal life and those around you.
- *you have a high regard for the human person*, because you believe that Jesus created us in His own image, that He died for us and that He came forth from the grave to reconcile His creation to God.
- *you believe the intrinsic value of humankind* demands the sacredness of all God's creation; you're the crowning achievement in God's plan.
- *you believe the grave is not the end.* You see life with a long–term view. And when things do not go the way you want, you know there is more to the story and you are willing to trust God with what you do not understand.

These are all things that most secular thinkers (Christian or otherwise) deny or are skeptical or confused about. But they are unmistakable signs of a biblical worldview.

WHAT'S THE POINT?: *There are some things that Jesus-thinkers don't agree on, but there are a few non–negotiables that draw a dividing line between believers and unbelievers.*

> **Secular thinkers believe mankind is inherently good. The Bible, history, and current events do not support that wishful thinking.**

PRAYER: *Dear Jesus, please teach me those Bible truths that are indispensable for Jesus followers. We have just one life to get it right. I want to make a difference by believing Your truth. Amen!*

INTERACT: How does your life stack up on the list of things that characterize Jesus thinkers who have a biblical worldview?

_____

_____

_____

- Are you confused or skeptical about any items on the above list? Which ones?

_____

_____

_____

_____

DAY 11
WHERE RUBBER MEETS ROAD

> "You then, my son, be strong in the grace that is in Christ Jesus. ²And the things you have heard me say in the presence of many witnesses entrust to reliable people who will also be qualified to teach others." —2 Timothy 2:1–2

By now you may be convinced of the benefits of thinking like Jesus. But you may also be stymied by the daunting task ahead. How do you become a Jesus thinker? There's no simple, paint–by–numbers formula for it, no one–size–fits–all. Each person is different. But there are many activities that can help the process along.

Start with prayer. This is foundational in your commitment to Being Like Jesus. Talking to God will crystalize your thinking over time. God already knows what you think, of course, but prayer is vital, and powerful, as Jesus leads us away from a lifetime of selfish thinking to a new way. Praying is commanded by God, so when you pray, you obey. That brings with it blessings and the favor of God.

Read through the whole Bible, read large sections, study a chapter, paragraph, sentence, verse, or word in–depth, using the Bible prompts. If you have read the Bible a lot, read 'unfamiliarly,' looking for new insights you haven't noticed before. As you read, ask God to help you understand and apply His truth to your daily life.

Examine your own life. Ask yourself often if you're thinking like Jesus. Seek the input of Christians you trust. Find a mentor and hold yourself accountable.

Develop new habits. Maybe it's less TV and video games, more exercise, more rest. Challenge yourself intellectually, try something new, take on challenges God could use to stretch and grow you mentally, emotionally, physically, spiritually or socially.

Set biblical goals. Read books on many subjects by great Christian writers. Memorize fundamental Scriptures. Listen to godly Christian podcasts. Take a Bible seminar or Masterclass®. Read Christian periodicals online, like *The Voice of the Martyrs* or *The Christian Post*, *World* magazine or *Christianity Today*.

The path to being like Jesus is a little different for each person. But God is cheering for you and devoted to your transformation. Follow His lead and enjoy the journey.

> "I am not today all that I hope to be, yet I see Jesus, and that assures me that I shall one day be like Him."
> —Charles Spurgeon

WHAT'S THE POINT?: *Becoming like Jesus takes work, sacrifice, and a price to pay, but oh, the rewards! Nothing is more important than going through life thinking, speaking, and acting like Jesus. It leads to success, satisfaction, and a life of joyful purpose.*

PRAYER: *Holy Spirit, please guide me as I follow up on my commitment to Being Like Jesus in my daily life. Thank You for Your help. Amen!*

INTERACT: Someone whom I believe is a Jesus thinker is:

_____

_____

That person has the tools to help me become more like Jesus ❐ Yes ❐ No

My favorite Christian book (or the one I want to read next) is:

_____

_____

Here's the next step in my plan to become more like Jesus:

_____

_____

DAY 12
WHAT DOES GOD NEED?

> "Anyone who loves their life will lose it, while anyone who hates their life in this world will keep it for eternal life. [26]Whoever serves me must follow me; and where I am, my servant also will be. My Father will honor the one who serves me."
> —John 12:25–26

> "...continue to work out your salvation with fear and trembling, [13]for it is God who works in you to will and to act in order to fulfill his good purpose."
> —Philippians 2:12b–13

Some may think they're doing God a favor by becoming a Jesus follower, and wonder, "What would God do without me? My loyalty to Him must fill a big, empty void in His life!" The truth is actually quite the opposite. God is doing us a favor the size of the universe!

In Philosophy 201, I struggled with the concept that to be infinite means God doesn't really need anything or anyone. He lacks nothing. It still annoys the ego sometimes to realize God doesn't need us as we need air, food, or sleep. God is complete without us. There's even pure fellowship between Father, Son, and Holy Spirit.

But God clearly *wants* a relationship with humankind. Even our own fallen nature would keep us from wanting God, if not for God putting the desire within us (Philippians 2:13).

"We can easily fall into the idolatrous notion that we may possess God. We never possess God; God possesses us. We do not grasp God; God grasps us. God transcends all our human theologizing. He will not be owned; He refuses to be controlled. He allows us to know Him only when we let Him grasp and possess us" (William P. Barker, *A Savior for All Seasons*).

While God doesn't literally *need* a relationship with us, He *wants* it. In fact, He sent Jesus, God the Son, to die a shameful death to take our death sentence. Then He rose to give us eternal life. The least we can do, in love and gratitude, is commit ourselves to think, speak, and act like Jesus.

> **We have nothing to lose, and everything to gain, by being like Jesus.**

WHAT'S THE POINT?: *Jesus has nothing to gain from a relationship with you. But He loves you, and wants a friendship with humankind. You, of course, have everything to gain and nothing to lose.*

PRAYER: *Thank You, precious Savior, for initiating a relationship with me. Show me how to bring a smile to Your face by the way I think, speak and act. Amen!*

INTERACT: Put the above quotation from *A Savior for All Seasons* into your own words here:

_____

_____

_____

God's desired relationship with you is a sign of His grace. What does that mean to you?

_____

_____

Describe an incident or situation you experienced where you can trace the connection between thinking, speaking, and acting:

_____

_____

2
WHAT IS GOD LIKE?

(Days 13-25)

To enrich your experience in Chapter Two, go to www.YouTube.com and watch "GOD Loves People More Than Anything!" (Point of Grace)

DAY 13
THE PIANO MICE

> "In the past God spoke to our ancestors through the prophets at many times and in various ways, ²but in these last days he has spoken to us by his Son, whom he appointed heir of all things, and through whom also he made the universe. ³The Son is the radiance of God's glory and the exact representation of his being, sustaining all things by his powerful word..."
> —Hebrews 1:1–3a

Jesus was one of the world's great storytellers. I like to think He might have told this one (if pianos had existed then), to connect God the Creator with His most–prized creation—you!

A family of mice once lived in a magnificent grand piano. Into their piano world came the majestic sounds of the regal instrument. It filled all the dark spaces with rich music and sweet harmonies. At first the mice were overwhelmed with awe. They drew comfort and strength from the thought that Someone—though invisible to them—made the music. He was close by, yet above, and beyond them. The gifted musician transcended their little piano–lives. They worshiped the Great Unseen Player who created the lovely melodies. They praised Him and spoke to each other of His loving greatness.

Then one day a daring mouse climbed up to another part of the piano. Soon he returned, thoughtful, and a little troubled. He had discovered how music was really made. Wires were the secret. Tightly stretched wires of graduated lengths and thicknesses trembled and vibrated when the music played. They must revise their old, outdated beliefs. None but the most ignorant mouse could any longer believe in the Great Unseen Player.

Later, another adventuresome explorer mouse carried the explanation to new heights. Hammers were the true secret, 88 felt–covered hammers dancing and leaping on the wires. This theory was more complicated, but it proved that they lived in a purely mechanical world of science. Let's hear no more about this mythical Great Musician. Any thinking mouse could see that there was nothing to the Player–Creator myth. He did not exist!

But the Great Unseen Player kept on playing anyway! And the mice still heard and enjoyed the spectacular music! Their unbelief did not change things so much, after all.

Like this family of piano–mice—through faith, or doubt, or unbelief—we are blessed by God's rich melodies and marvelous harmonies. They fill our lives each day. It's yet another reason to become more like Jesus. Call it grace!

WHAT'S THE POINT?: *Faithfully believing that God exists and knowing what He is like are essential if we are to be like Jesus. You may doubt God if you choose. But disbelief changes nothing. He still exists and continues* *to pour out love and blessings on you. Even a dedicated Jesus follower can benefit from pondering God's existence.*

PRAYER: *Thank You, Creator God, that even if someone doubts or denies Your existence, You continue to play the rich, beautiful music of life. Lord, I believe. Help my pockets of unbelief. Amen!*

> **You can wonder if God exists, but that doesn't change God. You may not believe in Him, but He believes in you.**

INTERACT: Describe a time someone disputed one of your beliefs about God:

_____

_____

_____

_____

Honest questions are useful for belief if you explore them with an open mind. What are some beliefs you have doubted or questioned in the past?

_____

_____

_____

_____

Here is one way that my past doubts have strengthened my faith:

_____

_____

_____

_____

When I realize that questions I may have about God do not change His love for me, I feel:

_____

_____

_____

_____

DAY 14

FINDING FAITH

> "Now faith is confidence in what we hope for and assurance about what we do not see… ⁶And without faith it is impossible to please God, because anyone who comes to him must believe that he exists and that he rewards those who earnestly seek him."
> —Hebrews 11:1, 6

In our quest to discover what God is like, it makes sense to probe the idea: Is God real? What does the Bible say? It is not silent about the existence of God, but neither does it objectively prove that God does exist. In his book, *Think Like Jesus*, George Barna writes, "…one of the most interesting discoveries I've made on my journey is that the Scriptures do not present a comprehensive, well-constructed argument regarding God's existence."

The Bible presents many concepts that are signs of the existence of God. But the Bible does not deal directly with the issue. The Bible assumes that you believe; it expects faith! Every Jesus follower believes, but reinforcement may be helpful.

Why has God allowed His very existence and His nature to be somewhat vague? He could have made His existence crystal clear, with no uncertainty, no doubts. For Him it would be easy-peasy! But for some reason He has chosen not to reveal irrefutable, empirical proof of His existence. He has purposely left His existence in some doubt, at least in some minds. He wants our faith to take hold and grow!

"Perhaps this is simply a tactic designed to nurture a meaningful relationship with us. It wouldn't be much of a relationship if He forced us into it. So, He waits to see what we will do. If we pursue Him, He is willing—yes, even *wanting*—to be found and to further reveal Himself to us," Barna writes. As today's Scripture says, God rewards all who earnestly seek for Him.

God is not some cosmic rapist who forces His affections on those who don't want Him. He longs for a relationship with you and me. But it must be a two-sided relationship. And our faith is key.

> God has left us to wrestle with this vital question of faith. He is willing to reveal Himself as we honestly search—and trust.

WHAT'S THE POINT?: *God could prove His existence easily. But that would ruin everything, because without faith it is impossible to please God. His proof remains shrouded because there is tremendous eternal value for those who decide to search. And He rewards the diligent searcher.*

PRAYER: *Thank You, Heavenly Father, for letting me use my mind and heart as resources to find and believe in You. Growing my faith is a noble and blessed process. Amen!*

INTERACT: God values faith more than proof. Think about a time you wished God would prove something, but He preferred that you live by faith instead.

_____

_____

_____

_____

The next time God's existence comes up, how can you emphasize the biblical truth that God values faith more than proof, even though He can prove anything?

_____

_____

_____

_____

Unbelievers mock faith, but use it all the time in their lives. What are a few examples of that everyday, mundane faith?

_____

_____

_____

_____

DAY 15

GAMES PEOPLE PLAY

> "The fool says in his heart, 'There is no God.' They are corrupt, and their ways are vile; there is no one who does good."
> —Psalm 53:1

Many sincere people have doubts about God. In many cases doubters are willing to believe. Remember the frantic father in Mark 9 whose son was possessed by demons? When Jesus said the boy could be healed if the father believed, he blurted, "I do believe; help me overcome my unbelief!" In this instance, Jesus was demonstrating that belief and uncertainty are surprisingly compatible.

Other people object to the very idea of a supreme being. If Jesus Christ, God the Son, walked into the room, they still would not believe He exists. Usually, the reason is less about lack of evidence than it is about accountability to the Supreme Being, *if* He actually exists.

The biblical evidence for God's existence is based on the idea that the reader already believes God exists, that the reader is a person of budding faith.

The Bible teaches that if you begin your quest for God from a position of faith, He will reveal Himself progressively in clear, unambiguous, and exciting ways.

The idea that we must have faith before God reveals Himself to us (In Latin it is said: *credendo vides*—"Believing is seeing!") is why so many find faith challenging. This matter of faith is fundamental. It is at the heart of being like Jesus. Understanding the nature of faith is essential in the process of becoming more like Jesus.

Disbelieving the Bible does not render the Bible untrue. It simply means you are refusing to submit yourself to God. Surrender is so hard for proud, self–absorbed people (i.e., pretty much all of us).

The absence or presence of faith is foundational to the worldview we have. If we are trying to develop a Christian worldview, there is no alternative. We *must* exercise faith!

WHAT'S THE POINT?: *Many people play a game with God: "Prove Your existence, then I'll decide whether I want to believe." God refuses to participate. Be willing to believe, then God will begin to reveal Himself to you.*

Most atheists refuse to believe God exists because if He does, they know they will have to submit to Him. Science isn't the issue, control is.

PRAYER: *The weak–kneed father said, "Lord, I believe. Help my unbelief"* (Mark 9:24). *Dear Savior, please bolster my faith so I can grow into who You had in mind when You created me. Amen!*

INTERACT: Recount an experience where you exercised faith, which led to seeing God's hand in your life.

_____

_____

_____

_____

Credendo vides i.e., "believing is seeing," has been evidenced in my life in this way:

_____

_____

_____

_____

Have you ever played this game with God: "Prove Your existence, then I will decide whether I want to believe"? How did that turn out for you?

_____
_____
_____
_____

I have known someone who refused to believe unless they saw physical evidence first. Here is how it turned out:

_____
_____
_____
_____

DAY 16
AN EXISTENTIAL CRISIS

> "The person without the Spirit does not accept the things that come from the Spirit of God but considers them foolishness, and cannot understand them because they are discerned only through the Spirit. [15]The person with the Spirit makes judgments about all things, but such a person is not subject to merely human judgments, [16]for, "Who has known the mind of the Lord so as to instruct him?" But we have the mind of Christ."
> —1 Corinthians 2:14–16

What does logic tell us about God's existence? And is logic enough to build our faith upon?

Few people realize that the idea, "All truth is subjective, or personal," is a product of our culture embracing anti–Christian ideals. In most Eastern religions (Hinduism, Buddhism, and so on) there is no "cognitive dissonance" when two opposite ideas are considered true.

Someone might say, "For you, God exists. For me, God is a myth!" That is a classic example of postmodern subjective thought. Does anyone actually believe, "For you, gravity exists. For me, gravity is a myth"? In the natural world, both of those propositions cannot be true. Why then do people believe that in the spiritual world, that line of reasoning is trustworthy?

Consider the ramifications. If God doesn't exist, but I believe He does, the future consequences are minimal. There is no one to whom I must answer for my mistaken belief. There is no penalty for faith.

On the other hand, if God does exist, but you don't believe it, the final consequences are terrifying! You will answer to the God of the universe for your unbelief.

While this reasoning alone is not a sufficient basis for believing that God exists, it is a powerful motivation on the side of faith.

WHAT'S THE POINT?: *Postmodern subjective thought is illogical and does not agree with truth as stated in God's word, or evidenced in the natural world. The existential risk falls entirely on the side of unbelief. One should weigh this carefully when choosing to become more like Jesus.*

> **The risks inherent in postmodern subjectivity are alarming. If I don't believe in God but He does exist, I have painted myself into a corner with no way out.**

PRAYER: *Lord God, please transform my thinking so that I am consistent with what You say is truth. Amen!*

INTERACT: Here is how I would contrast spiritually discerned judgments with "merely human judgments" (1 Corinthians 2:15).

_____
_____
_____
_____

What's the difference in decision making between the person who has the "mind of Christ," and one who relies on secular ideas to make life decisions?

_____
_____
_____

Why can human logic be a minefield when making decisions about life?

_____
_____
_____
_____

How would you describe the results of a core value that proclaims, "All truth is subjective, or personal?"

DAY 17

THE MOSAIC OF PROOF

> "Simon Peter answered, 'You are the Messiah, the Son of the living God.' [17]Jesus replied, 'Blessed are you, Simon son of Jonah, for this was not revealed to you by flesh and blood, but by my Father in heaven. [18]And I tell you that you are Peter, and on this rock I will build my church, and the gates of Hades will not overcome it.'"
> —Matthew 16:16–18

What do church traditions say about the reality of God? They are the time–honored insights of godly people through history. And why do they matter in the pursuit of Being Like Jesus?

While church traditions support the conclusion that God is indeed real, they're not authoritative on a level with the Word of God. And if traditions disagree with the Bible, they are dangerous. Church traditions can still be useful for understanding how God has interacted with His human creation through history.

Church traditions declare the reality of God and have chronicled His personal connections with people of faith for millennia. They must always align with the Bible, but they still help us see how, through the ages, God, His creation and humanity have interacted in relationship together.

What can we learn from *personal experience?* Though not authoritative in the biblical sense, this is the area of proof that many rely upon most. This includes those whose personal experience has not involved the pursuit of God.

Many of us can answer the question, "How have you encountered and experienced God in your personal life?" You may have stories of miracles God has done; some have actually heard God's voice; or maybe

He speaks to you through a trusted Pastor or friend. Most can recount times we have experienced God through His natural creation.

You must be careful, of course, because *human experience is utterly useless when employed as a judge against God Himself.* Many have been ruined by elevating their own subjective experiences above Scripture, church tradition and the wisdom of godly people. As you share your faith with those who struggle, steer them away from speculation about traditions and toward more practical ways to develop and grow their emerging faith. There's plenty of time for them to consider the less essential principles of church tradition in another setting.

WHAT'S THE POINT?: *The orthodox traditions of the church can reinforce the teachings of Scripture and logic. Personal experience is also useful in forming one's beliefs about God. They are both pieces in the mosaic of proof for the reality of God.*

> **The Christian church, personal experience, and godly advice all contribute to becoming like Jesus.**

PRAYER: *Blessed Lord, if You didn't exist, I wouldn't exist. Thank You for creating such a beautiful world and people who care about me. Amen!*

INTERACT: When Peter said, "You are the Messiah, the Son of the living God" (Matthew 16:16), it was a radical idea to his culture and carried a death sentence. What are some parallels to the same claim today?

_____

_____

_____

_____

How would you refute the idea that Jesus said, "I will build My church on Peter, the rock"? On what was Jesus saying He would build His church?

_____

_____

_____

Does your church have any traditions that are not based in Scripture? If so, what are they and what might you do about it?

_____

_____

_____

I have seen the danger of relying on personal experience to judge a Bible teaching. It was

_____

_____

_____

DAY 18
WANTED DEAD OR ALIVE

> "If you declare with your mouth, 'Jesus is Lord,' and believe in your heart that God raised him from the dead, you will be saved. [10]For it is with your heart that you believe and are justified, and it is with your mouth that you profess your faith and are saved...[13]for, "Everyone who calls on the name of the Lord will be saved."
> —Romans 10:9, 10, 13

So maybe God did exist at one time, some claimed. Maybe He is now dead! Such a discussion is worthy of anyone seeking to become like Jesus. The answer impacts the search for what God is like. If He's dead, the whole idea is moot.

In the 1960s, when I was a teenager, there was a short–lived movement in liberal religious circles that trumpeted, "God is dead!" There were at least two leaders of this movement. Episcopal Bishop James Pike had many life problems. He was married three times and reportedly had numerous adulterous affairs. He had a persistent drinking problem, yet was elected a Bishop. He died in 1969 while wandering aimlessly in the Israeli desert, searching for a son who had taken his own life. Pike brazenly proclaimed that God had died, literally.

Thomas Althizer, a professor at Emory University in Atlanta, Georgia, made headlines by insisting that the God of tradition was no longer relevant—that is, the traditional God was dead. These two were point men in the "God is dead!" movement. They gained a small amount of fleeting fame for their insistence that in a modern age, with a society that had evolved, it was no longer possible to believe in the traditional Christian God.

By the end of the tumultuous 1960s, "God is Dead" was on its way to the cemetery. But the God of the Bible survived. He could say, like Mark Twain, "Reports of My demise are greatly exaggerated!"

Pike's and Althizer's personal experiences tainted their beliefs. Proverbs 14:12 may have been written with them in mind: "There is a way that seems right to a man, but in the end, it leads to death!"

While personal experience may accompany us to stronger faith, it may also erode our faith if trusted too explicitly. Tragedy awaits if you elevate human experience and ideas above other evidence for God's existence (1 Corinthians chapter 1).

Entire libraries could be filled with tomes debating the reality of God. Few subjects have generated as much heat as this one—though not always much light. But there is much compelling evidence for God's literal existence.

People of faith insist, a real, loving, righteous God does exist and He wants a personal, intimate relationship with His people. That's the practical aspect of thinking about the reality of God.

> A song that provides truth here is YouTube.com: The Newsboys' "God's Not Dead" lyrics

WHAT'S THE POINT?: *Life experiences are a poor basis for faith, since every life has many sources of input besides God. His existence is a vital principle even for believers. Being objective about life is extremely difficult. Even Jesus' followers wrestle with it. Yet a life of faith is the best life, as eternity will prove.*

PRAYER: *Father, Son, and Holy Spirit, I believe You are the living God. I commit myself to being like You and telling my sphere of influence that You are alive and well. Amen!*

INTERACT: I have seen the practical truth of Proverbs 14:12 in real life. Here's the story:

In Romans 10:10, does Paul mean we earn our salvation in part by witnessing for Jesus? Why or why not?

___

___

___

___

Where does your human experience fit with other evidence for a living God?

___

___

___

___

A few great books on faith in God are, *I Don't Have Enough Faith to Be An Atheist* (Geisler & Turek); *Reflections on the Existence of God* (Richard E. Simmons III); *The Case for FAITH* (Lee Strobel); *and What Good is God?* (Philip Yancey). And there are many others. I plan to read the following books after I finish reading *Being Like Jesus*.

___

___

___

___

DAY 19

PEEKING BEHIND THE CURTAIN

> "'For my thoughts are not your thoughts, neither are your ways my ways,' declares the LORD. ⁹'As the heavens are higher than the earth, so are my ways higher than your ways and my thoughts than your thoughts.'"
> —Isaiah 55:8–9

When human beings ask, "What is God like?" can they expect an adequate answer? In one respect, God and His most favored creation are worlds apart, literally. As long ago as 750 BC, God pointed out through the prophet Isaiah that He is far above us. While humans are at the apex of creation, God is light years above and beyond. He is transcendent.

Yes, God's thoughts are high above ours. Yet there are things about God we can know. For example, consider the aspect of God's essence. *He is pure spirit. Humankind is a hybrid physical and spiritual being.* Though we are different from, and subject to God, we share in His essence in numerous ways.

We were created in His intellectual image. We can reason. We can use logic to solve problems. We can think about motives for what we do. We can predict results from our actions and anticipate expected results from decisions we might make.

We share God's moral nature. We can reflect on right and wrong, though the sin nature corrupts these concepts from birth. We need God's Word, the Bible, to transform our thinking about right and wrong, good and bad. We can reason out the consequences of our actions, unlike animals who must be trained to act in certain ways (as in Pavlovian or Skinner–esque behavioral conditioning).

We are capable of intimacy on a higher, spiritual level. The hybrid physical–spiritual being can worship a purely spiritual God because we are made in His image.

We have the God–like capacity for creativity. We may marvel at nature, artistic endeavor or engineering feats resulting from God's creative image in mankind.

What is God like? He's a God of transcendent, inspiring awe. Study Him for a lifetime (*theology* is two Greek words meaning 'God' and 'word' or 'learning') and you will be increasingly aware of how little humankind can comprehend the unequaled God of the universe Who is so high above us. Yet God wants us to know and love Him.

WHAT'S THE POINT?: *You can discern a partial answer to "What is God Like?" by looking around you and considering humankind and the rest of God's creation. Of course, God exceeds all of His creation, and awe is an appropriate response to an even limited grasp of God.*

> "God dwells in His creation and is ... present in all His works. He is transcendent above all His works even while He [resides] within them."
> —A. W. Tozer

PRAYER: *Lord, as my life unfolds, show me how great and superior You are. Please give me a thirst for You and Your magnificence. Amen!*

INTERACT: Which of the five things we can know about God's nature, listed above, most inspires and encourages you?

_____

_____

_____

_____

What are a few of God's qualities that humankind does not share?
_____
_____
_____
_____

An example of my thoughts and ways being far below God's is:
_____
_____
_____
_____

I want to enhance one quality I share with God's nature. It is:
_____
_____
_____
_____

DAY 20
GOD IS THE CEO!?!?!

> [Jesus said] "You *Samaritans* worship what you do not know; we worship what we do know, because salvation is from the Jews. [23] But a time is coming, and even now has arrived, when the true worshipers will worship the Father in spirit and truth; for such people the Father seeks *to be* His worshipers. [24] God is spirit, and those who worship Him must worship in spirit and truth."
> —John 4:22–24 (NASB)

God's essence may seem mysterious and impenetrable. But as today's Scripture says, there is a practical application to grappling with the concept of God's nature. That practicality is worship.

In *Man: Ruined and Restored,* author Leslie Flynn identified four qualities related to God's essence. First, humanity's assignment of stewardship over the rest of creation is akin to *God's rule.* Someone explained this as God being the corporate CEO. His fellow workers are the managers and the foremen of various work crews, with supervision of thousands, hundreds, tens. Then there are the rank–and–file workers who do the scutwork. Don't forget, Jesus, God among us, taught us to humbly wash the disciples' feet. With varying levels of responsibility, each believer has tasks to accomplish under God's rule.

Second, *humans are rational beings,* like our Creator. The rest of creation is not. Aside from the subordinate level humans occupy under the headship of God and His created messengers, the angels, this rationality is a major component of being like Jesus.

One definition of righteousness is, "Right living according to God's Word." The third quality of God's essence is *the innate need to live the right way*. Despite the chaotic noise of voices telling us the world's view of "right living," God is the one to heed.

Fourth, *God created us to function in relationships* on many levels, the first being our relationship with Him. The perfect fellowship between God the Father, Son, and Holy Spirit is a model for all human relationships.

God's essence is spirit, which complicates the interaction from our side of the street. But it doesn't mean that God isn't real, just because we cannot see or hear Him with the usual senses.

> **Knowing about God's rule, rationality, righteousness and relationships provides a framework to continue the quest for "What is God like?"**

WHAT'S THE POINT?: *Understanding God's nature reinforces faith in Him. Being Like Jesus compels us to grow in our comprehension of God the Father, Son and Holy Spirit.*

PRAYER: *The more I understand what You're like, Jesus, the more I want to follow You. Please help my search for You. Amen!*

INTERACT: Once you develop a greater appreciation of God's essence (or *nature*), how is your faith reinforced?

_____
_____
_____

What's involved in being a "true worshiper of God" in a.) spirit; and in b.) truth (John 4:23)?

_____
_____
_____
_____

I aspire to this level of leadership in Jesus's "corporation." Here's what I will do to achieve that:

_____

_____

_____

_____

DAY 21
THE G.O.A.T.

> "Here is a trustworthy saying that deserves full acceptance: Christ Jesus came into the world to save sinners—of whom I [Paul] am the worst. ¹⁶ But for that very reason I was shown mercy so that in me, the worst of sinners, Christ Jesus might display his immense patience as an example for those who would believe in him and receive eternal life. ¹⁷ Now to the King eternal, immortal, invisible, the only God, be honor and glory for ever and ever. Amen."
> —1 Timothy 1:15–17

There's a new term in sports. They say Muhammad Ali, Tom Brady, and Michael Jordan deserve the GOAT label. The goat used to be the player who dropped the touchdown pass or struck out with the bases loaded. Today the GOAT is the Greatest Of All Time.

As we ponder what God is like, we are confronted with both His essence, or nature, and His greatness. In this context, His "greatness" can signify the biggest, best, strongest, most effective, superlative beyond words.

For many decades, Marvel, DC Comics, George Lucas and others have been designing and building superheroes who want to be the GOAT. But so far, not one has been able to forgive sins and make you or me right with God. That's a miracle confined only to Jesus.

Wanna become a Jesus follower? Even the most phenomenal superhero cannot compare to the perfection of greatness that is God in Christ Jesus.

His *wisdom* is beyond the human ability to comprehend. His *power* dwarfs the largest nuclear device. His *accomplishments* eclipse the greatest feats in human history.

God's greatness is proven by His *omnipresence*; He is everywhere at once. "Where can I go from your Spirit?" King David asked. "Where can I flee from your presence? If I go up to the heavens, you are there; if I make my bed in the depths, you are there" (Psalm 139:7–8). God's omnipresence is either a wonderful thing (He is always within reach to help you) or a terrible thing (you can run but you can't hide).

Another aspect of God's greatness is, *He is personal.* This is not the Deist's God who created us, then lost interest, or turned away to pursue other hobbies.

The pinnacle of God's personal nature is *His gift of salvation* through Jesus Christ. Evidence of His commitment to personal relationships is that He came and lived, suffered, sweated, worked, and finally died and rose again, even for those who will never decide to follow Him. How great is that?*

What is God like? He is a God of inexpressible greatness. You'd have more success holding back Niagara Falls with a teaspoon than describing the dimensions of God's greatness.

WHAT'S THE POINT?: *God is undoubtedly the Greatest Of All Time. He transcends time and space, eternity and the universe. And He deeply desires a relationship with you! Which means, being like Jesus is the best anyone could ever wish to be! Life doesn't get any better than that!*

> "God's glory matters more than anything. If people don't know how great and gracious and good He is... How will they know He's better than everything else..."
> —Louie Giglio

PRAYER: *God of the universe, please give me just a glimpse of how great You are. Truly, You transcend the Greatest Of All Time. Amen!*

INTERACT: God has displayed His immense patience (1 Timothy 1:16) in me, one of the worst of sinners. Here's what I mean:

_____
_____
_____
_____

A powerful glimpse of God's greatness is:

_____
_____
_____
_____

Does the knowledge that you can never escape God's presence comfort or worry you? Explain why:

_____
_____
_____
_____

Briefly describe your intimate relationship with God:

_____
_____
_____
_____

*Reformed theology teaches that Jesus died only for those who are the select, who will ultimately accept His sacrifice and appropriate His offer of salvation. Free Will theology claims that God wants to save every person in the world, and redeems everyone who decides to trust Jesus as Savior. God loves and blesses people on both sides of the coin.

DAY 22
GOD OF PLAN B

> "God is light; in him there is no darkness at all. ⁶If we claim to have fellowship with him and yet walk in the darkness, we lie and do not live out the truth. ⁷But if we walk in the light, as he is in the light, we have fellowship with one another, and the blood of Jesus, his Son, purifies us from all sin."
> —1 John 1:5–7

How do goodness and greatness differ? If God is robed in greatness, is it a foregone conclusion that God is also good? Michael Jordan, Tom Brady, and Muhammad Ali were perhaps the greatest in their chosen sports. That does not necessarily mean they are also good people. The two concepts differ in their nature. *Great* and *good* are different in their very essence.

God is both great and good—great in His nature, good in His actions and interactions with His creation.

God is very good to all who acknowledge Him. He is even good to many who reject Him. He's holy, morally pure, and completely without sin.

God is light, and in Him there is no darkness. The Bible says people hate light because they want to hide their evil ways. Being like Jesus means we cherish the goodness of light as a facet of what God is like.

On a trip to Africa, I took along the Child Evangelism Fellowship™ wordless book, made up of colorful pages. One page is black to signify sin, another is white to signify God's cleansing. As I was sharing that book one day in an African school, I mentioned that black was bad and white was good. Then I saw seventy black African students staring at me. I realized with a jolt, it is more accurate—and compassionate—to say the "darkness" of sin is bad and "clean" is good.

God is love, which goes beyond "God is loving." It means He is the source, the very essence of unselfish, others–first love. When Jesus died for your sins, His love gave Himself up for your best.

He is the very definition of faithfulness. He always stays true to His perfect nature (this is one of the best definitions of *integrity*, by the way). He is utterly dependable, the same yesterday, today and forever (Hebrews 13:8).

What is God like? *He values grace above all*. It is His *modus operandi*. Most secular thinkers believe God is all about judgment. Asked to define 'Christian,' they list what they think we are against. But God's nature is to give grace, those wonderful blessings we do not deserve and cannot earn! In His goodness, God saves us by His grace.

God is patience personified. He believes in us and bears with us far longer than we would. When we mess up plan A, He is the God of plan B.

> **God shines sunlight on the evil and the good; it rains on both good and bad farmers. Most never realize how much they benefit from God's goodness.**

WHAT'S THE POINT?: *We're learning to think like Jesus about God the Trinity. His nature, His very essence, is supreme goodness.*

PRAYER: *Lord Jesus, as I surrender to your Spirit to be more like You, reflecting the goodness of God, please lead me. Amen!*

INTERACT: "All who do evil hate the light and refuse to go near it for fear their sins will be exposed" (John 3:20 NLT). I am hiding this sin from the light of day:

_____
_____
_____
_____

Give a life example for one or more facets of Jesus's goodness (light, love, faithfulness, grace, patience):

_____

_____

_____

_____

If you asked an acquaintance to define "Christian," based on you, what would they say?

_____

_____

_____

_____

DAY 23

WHAT REALLY, REALLY MATTERS

> "His divine power has given us everything we need for a godly life through our knowledge of him who called us by his own glory and goodness. ⁴ Through these he has given us his very great and precious promises, so that through them you may participate in the divine nature, having escaped the corruption in the world caused by evil desires."
> —2 Peter 1:3–4

The Library of Congress might not be able to contain all the writings, throughout human history, about God's existence and nature. The subject has fascinated mankind and has frustrated all efforts to prove or disprove it, empirically. But a probing question remains: Does your belief really matter?

Today's Scripture shows that humankind is without excuse for unbelief, because God has provided all we need for life and godliness. God will hold us accountable for what we do with the evidence. Romans 1:18–20 warns of His anger toward all who "push the truth away from themselves." What more powerful reason to pursue faith do you need? Resolving our questions about God's existence and what He is like should top our bucket list.

Through God's great and precious promises, Peter wrote, we may participate in the divine nature, maybe the most astonishing promise in all of human experience. That is not saying everyone is a part of god and god is a part of everything, as eastern religions tout. That belittles God. But to share in His nature (finding and developing godly qualities) is a profound, though sobering, possibility. And a treasure beyond earthly value. That's what makes Being Like Jesus realistically attainable!

On the day you stand before Him to account for your faith or disbelief, He will accept no excuses for rebellion or rejection. If Father God has revealed Himself through nature, through the Scriptures, through God the Son, Jesus, and through human experience, neither ignorance nor unbelief will get you off the hook.

WHAT'S THE POINT?: *Faith matters supremely. Being like Jesus is the only safe and satisfying way to spend this lifetime and all eternity.*

Go to YouTube.com and find this song: It will bless you . . . "Breathe" by Michael W Smith

PRAYER: *Lord, may my pursuit of You be my highest priority. Please help me stay on target and not be sidetracked by less important things. Amen!*

INTERACT: How do believers who claim God's promises get to participate in His divine nature?

_____

_____

_____

_____

If you were to purge all belief in God from your mind and heart, how would your life be different?

_____

_____

_____

Paint a word picture of the "corruption in the world caused by evil desires" (2 Peter 1:4):

_____
_____
_____

_____

Cite evidence that you're desperate and lost without God:

_____
_____
_____
_____

DAY 24
THE 'F' WORD

> "Now faith is confidence in what we hope for and assurance about what we do not see. ²This is what the ancients were commended for. ³By faith we understand that the universe was formed at God's command, so that what is seen was not made out of what was visible... ⁶And without faith it is impossible to please God..."
> —Hebrews 11:1–3, 6a

Faith in God is fundamental to the Christian worldview. You can't have one without the other. And, you can't be like Jesus without deep, lasting faith. If your goal is "Being Like Jesus," you must believe not only that God exists, but also that He is the kind of God who will reward your honest spiritual search.

Often those who set out to prove God is not real by digging into the Bible and Christian philosophers, end up believing. One such person was journalist Lee Strobel, whose journey to faith commenced after a Christian nurse saved their child from choking at a restaurant, and his wife came to faith. Strobel was determined to prove that God does not exist. Instead, by the end of his search he embraced God, and went on to write such classics as *The Case for Faith, The Case for Christ, The Case for a Creator,* and others. He was transformed from atheist to Christian apologist. He has touched the world for Jesus. Faith made all the difference in Lee Strobel's life. His journey to faith is told in the film, *The Case for Christ*.

We're compelled to believe that God will bless our desire and efforts to be like Jesus by developing a Christian worldview.

Being like Jesus means we surrender to the King of kings, the Lord of lords, Who is Master of the universe. Subduing self is one of the hardest things a human being can do. In the Old Testament an army commander refused to be healed of leprosy because he couldn't humble himself just a little (2 Kings chapter 5).

When you approach the Lord as the human Jesus did here on Earth, you will be moving toward developing the mind of Christ in your daily life.

Acknowledging that God is Who He says He is means you must admit, "He is God and I am NOT!"

WHAT'S THE POINT?: *When we think like Jesus, success, satisfaction and living on purpose will guide us to make a difference for God. They will enrich our lives, and help us make the world a better place.*

PRAYER: *Lord God, thank You for helping me along the path to greater faith. Please reward my search for You. Amen!*

INTERACT: Look up *creation ex nihilo* to explain how God made the universe.

_____
_____
_____

What does an evolutionist say when asked where the first matter which became the universe originated (Hebrews 11:3)?

_____
_____
_____

Do you know anyone who transformed from atheist to Christian believer? How can their story help you and others?

_____
_____

WHAT IS GOD LIKE?

_____

_____

I have recently progressed toward Jesus thinker in this way:

_____

_____

_____

_____

DAY 25

WHAT *HE* SAID

> [Jesus said] "Your father Abraham rejoiced at the thought of seeing my day; he saw it and was glad." ⁵⁷'You are not yet fifty years old,' they said to him, 'and you have seen Abraham!' ⁵⁸'Very truly I tell you,' Jesus answered, 'before Abraham was born, I AM!'"
> —John 8:56–58

The actor Cary Grant was walking along a street and met a man going the other way. They made eye contact and the man said excitedly, "Aren't you...you're—I know who you are; don't tell me—uh, Rock Hudson...No, you're..."

The famous actor thought he had better help the poor guy, so he finished the man's sentence: "I'm Cary Grant."

The other fellow replied, "No, that's not it. Just let me think... You're—!"

Did Cary Grant cease to exist because the fellow refused to believe he was who he said he was? Of course not.

The Creator of the universe meets up with a woman, and she says, "I know You. You're..." When she can't come up with it, God helps her. "I'm God!" He replies. The woman says, "No, that's not it...Just give me a minute!"

It's almost comical, the lengths to which many will go to avoid acknowledging God for who He says He is. They use dubious science, psychology, nature worship, even a soulmate, to fill the God–shaped void and bolster their belief that God is a myth, the Bible one long fable, and the answers to life can be found within themselves.

If you are a seeker, not a believer, I invite you to acknowledge God for Who He says He is. See Him through faith as He really is. Commit yourself to become one of His children. Determine to think, speak, and act like Jesus. It's the beginning of a wonderful life of success, satisfaction, and living on purpose!

WHAT'S THE POINT?: *What God has said in the Scripture is trustworthy. It makes no sense to put your faith in failed human ideas when God has given you His divine word. Trust Him and start looking a lot like Jesus.*

> Few have enough faith to be an atheist. It is easier to believe in God as Creator than to put your faith in the failed philosophies of the world's "wise" guys.

PRAYER: *Father in heaven, transform my mind to weigh Your wisdom against the world's, then choose Your best path for me. Amen!*

INTERACT: How do Jesus's words, "Before Abraham was, I AM!" impact your life?

___

___

___

___

As the culture seeks to cancel God, how are they successful or unsuccessful?

___

___

___

___

I think that acknowledging God for who He says He is will enhance my success, satisfaction and purpose in this way:

___

___

___

___

3

GOD OF WONDERS, BEYOND OUR GALAXY

(Days 26–37)

To enrich your experience in Chapter Three, go to www.YouTube.com and listen to "Because of Who You Are" by Sandi Patti

DAY 26

CREATIVITY AT A PREMIUM

> "For in him all things were created: things in heaven and on earth, visible and invisible, whether thrones or powers or rulers or authorities; all things have been created through him and for him. [17] He is before all things, and in him all things hold together."
> —Colossians 1:16–17

Unsurprisingly, many American Christians would benefit from a more recognizable Christian worldview. The Catholic clergy aside, George Barna has discovered that only half of American Protestant pastors have a Biblical worldview.*

We would define such a worldview as believing that absolute moral truth exists, and that right and wrong are defined by God in the Bible. We embrace a biblical view on six core beliefs: the accuracy of biblical teaching, the sinless nature of Jesus, the literal existence of Satan, the all-knowing and all-powerful God, salvation by grace alone, and a personal responsibility to evangelize the lost (see Day 10).

If half of America's Protestant pastors have a secular worldview, how can we expect the church to lead the restoration of our nation?

In the online *The Christian Post* edition of January 27, 2023, Richard D. Land observed, "If the *pastors*, the shepherds of the flock, have succumbed to subbiblical worldviews, who is going to lead the people and 'teach them all things whatsoever I have commanded you'?" (Matthew 8:18-20).

In a remote Swiss village stood a beautiful mountain valley cathedral. It had the most beautiful pipe organ in the region. People would come from far and near to hear the lovely organ. Then an eerie silence descended. Something was wrong. Experts from around the world were summoned to repair the organ. No one was successful.

One day an older man appeared and asked to try his hand. For two days the old man worked in almost total silence. The sexton was getting nervous. On the third day the Alpine valley once again resonated with heavenly music.

After the older man finished playing, someone asked how he could restore this magnificent instrument when even the world's experts had failed. He merely said, "It was I who created this organ, and now I have restored it."

The God of Creation, who created you and me, wants to restore us. And He wants to do that by teaching us to be like Jesus! Humanity, broken and discordant, needs the hand of the Master Creator to restore us to harmony with Himself and others, and the world around us.

WHAT'S THE POINT?: *Being like Jesus means we will embrace God as Creator, and worship Him for the many facets of His handiwork. Trusting God like this will result in success, satisfaction and living on purpose.*

> **Comparing truth from the Bible and the claims of truth from secular sources, I'll take my chances with the Lord of heaven and Earth.**

PRAYER: *Dear Lord, please show me the genius of Your creation. Thank You for making such a magnificent natural world for us to enjoy. Amen!*

INTERACT: About whom was Paul writing in today's Scripture reading?

_____

_____

_____

_____

For what two specific acts is he responsible, according to Colossians 1:16–17?

_____

_____

_____

_____

I believe many church leaders ❏ have ❏ do not have Bible-based worldviews, based on this observation:

_____

_____

_____

_____

What does the Master Creator need to do to restore you to, or begin, thinking like Jesus?

_____

_____

_____

_____

* (Michael Foust posted this finding on Metadata, January 14, 2004) Barna: Only half of nation's senior pastors hold biblical worldview, www.baptistpress.com

DAY 27
ODE TO CREATION

> "When I consider your heavens, the work of your fingers, the moon and the stars, which you have set in place, ⁴what is man that you are mindful of him, the son of man that you care for him? ⁵You made him a little lower than the heavenly beings and crowned him with glory and honor. ⁶You made him ruler over the works of your hands; you put everything under his feet."
> —Psalm 8:3–6

A close examination of King David's anthem to God's creative genius (Psalm 8) can take your breath away. First, there is the orderly structure of the poem. Notice this Psalm's symmetry, balance, and mirror image. English and Gaelic poets taught us that poetry should rhyme and have even meter. Not so with Hebrew poetry. Comparison, contrast, restatement, mirror image, and especially symmetry are the things. If you are a word person, Psalm 8 sparkles with beauty and shimmers with discovery. Here is a common diagram of its chiastic structure (emphasizing reverse order):

    a. God's excellent name (8:1)
    b. God's rule in creation (8:2, 3)
    c. Man's lowliness, in his own view (8:4)
    c. Man's greatness, in God's view (8:5)
    b. Man's rule in creation (8:6–8)
    a. God's excellent name (8:9)

Next, ponder the themes of Psalm 8. David emphasized the attributes of God's character qualities, evident by the typically Hebrew usage of the word 'name' (8:1, 9). Then there is the broad sweep of creation:

God's involvement and humankind's response (8:2, 3, 6–8). And do not miss humankind's relationship to God and His creation (8:4–5).

Ultimately, this Psalm guides the reader to think like Jesus. God is so wonderful; He is beyond imagining. His greatness is displayed in the marvels of His masterpiece. Why should the divine, sovereign God pay any attention to lowly humankind? But wait: God views humanity as the pinnacle of His creation, third only to God Himself and the angels in the hierarchy of the universe.

God has placed creation into human hands for management and for enjoyment. As shown by His character, isn't God more magnificent than we can even express?

Understanding Psalm 8 sets the table for the devotionals on Days 28 and 29, which follow.

> "Thou hast made us for thyself, O Lord, and our heart is restless until it finds its rest in thee."
> —St. Augustine of Hippo, *Confessions*

WHAT'S THE POINT?: *God has entrusted His creation into human hands because He has high regard for us. Worship Him and treat His craftsmanship with care.*

PRAYER: *Dear Lord Jesus, I am grateful for Your work of creating the universe. Please show me how to take great care of it. Amen!*

INTERACT: Lord, help me "sing Your Song of Creation" like this to influence others:

_____

_____

_____

_____

I will do this to manage and enjoy God's creative masterpiece:

_____

_____

_____

_____

The fact that God the Father loves lowly, yet exalted, humankind enough to sacrifice His special, Son, Jesus, shows me that:

_____

_____

_____

_____

DAY 28

THIS, THAT, AND THE OTHER

> "So God created mankind in his own image, in the image of God he created them; male and female he created them. ²⁸God blessed them and said to them, 'Be fruitful and increase in number; fill the earth and subdue it. Rule over the fish in the sea and the birds in the sky and over every living creature that moves on the ground.' ³¹God saw all that he had made, and it was very good. And there was evening, and there was morning—the sixth day." —Genesis 1:27–28, 31

Taken at face value, the idea that God created by using Darwinian evolutionary principles contains a fatal discrepancy.* Either everything came into being through natural selection. Or creation happened by the hand of God, as the Bible says. One or the other, but not both. If you embrace the Bible as God's self-revelation, Darwin must have been way out in left field.

Why do so many hold onto evolution with a death grip? It might have little to do with science. If there is a Creator and He made the universe specifically, as reported in Genesis, it changes everything in deniers' lives. He is the Supreme Being and they would be accountable to Him. That's a situation to be avoided more than COVID-19.

C.S. Lewis wrote in *Mere Christianity* that out of the human attempt to minimize or discard God "has come nearly all that we call human history...the long terrible story of a man trying to find something other than God which will make him happy."

Evolutionists like to refer to that moment when creation began (merely by chance, of course) as The Big Bang. Louie Giglio says when God opened His mouth and spoke the universe into being, you can be confident there was a really big bang!

WHAT'S THE POINT?: *Either God created the World as the Bible asserts, or everything evolved. There can be no dichotomy in the origin of species.*

PRAYER: *God, I embrace You as the Maker of everything that exists. And I surrender to Your supremacy. Amen!*

> "A house testifies that there was a builder, a dress that there was a weaver; a door that there was a carpenter; so, our world by its existence proclaims its Creator, God."
> —Rabbi Akiba ben Joseph

INTERACT: In Genesis 1:28, what did God mean in His instruction to "subdue" the earth and rule over every living creature?

_____
_____
_____
_____

I believe that the Bible is God's self-revelation. That belief motivates me to:

_____
_____
_____
_____

Check out the powerful teachings in C.S. Lewis's *Mere Christianity*.

_____
_____
_____
_____

*For a fuller treatment of this subject from a Christian worldview, search the Internet for "*The Six Days of Creation and Evolutionary Theory: Compatible?* | *Answers in Genesis*" by Philip du Toit & Callie Joubert, November 23, 2011, Featured in *Answers in Depth*.

DAY 29

MICRO VERSUS MACRO

> "This is what God the Lord says—the Creator of the heavens, who stretches them out, who spreads out the earth with all that springs from it, who gives breath to its people, and life to those who walk on it: ⁶"I, the Lord, have called you in righteousness; I will take hold of your hand. I will keep you and will make you to be a covenant for the people and a light for the Gentiles." —Isaiah 42:5–6

Nineteenth-century American sculptor Emma Stebbins wrote, "To me, it seems as if when God conceived the world, that was poetry; he formed it, and that was sculpture; he colored it, and that was painting; he peopled it with living beings, and that was the grand, divine, eternal drama."

There are two main theories of origins. They are "theories" because the scientific method asserts that if a belief cannot be verified by experimentation and duplication, it is only a theory, not a fact. Neither evolution nor biblical creation can be verified by experimentation or repetition.

These two theories are in complete contrast with one another. The Bible's explanation of creation is plainly stated if you take time to examine it carefully. God spoke, and the universe came into being *ex nihilo*—out of nothing. Try that, you evolutionists.

On the other hand, a theory embraced by virtually all atheists and a majority of scientists and educators, claims that all existing organisms came about by the process of many chronological, minuscule, meaningless alterations over millions of years.

Darwin left a back door exit open, but most Darwinians today find it chained and padlocked. He wrote, "If it could be demonstrated that any complex organ existed which could not possibly have been formed by numerous, successive, slight modifications, my theory would absolutely break down" (*On the Origin of Species by Means of Natural Selection*: Bantam Classic, 1999, p. 158).

I was discussing this subject once with a friend who believes Genesis chapters one and two took millions of years because of all the extremely old stuff there is on Earth. I said, "If God is truly divine, He *could* create something that was instantly a million years old. No problemo."

"No," he exclaimed, "that would be dishonest of God."

I ask you, "Do you think God created Adam as a neonatal infant one second old?" Well, of course not. Jesus Christ, who is both one hundred percent God and one hundred percent human, can make something *brand new* that is also *eons old*. I couldn't, you couldn't, but God can. And I believe He did.

There are two levels of evolution: Microevolution (change and adaptation within a species); and Macroevolution (one species gives rise to a completely different species).

The Christian worldview easily allows for microevolution. Many examples of adaptation are found in nature. The notion that one species becomes another violates the report of Scripture (grass, herbs, and fruit reproduce "after its kind" Gen. 1:11–12). In fact, evolutionist scientists are still looking for the missing link. It is missing because God, the Creator, did not create it.

WHAT'S THE POINT?: *Microevolution (adaptation) is yet another evidence of the Creator. Macroevolution (species change) is evidence of people desperate to be rid of the Creator.*

PRAYER: *God of the universe, You are my King; I am Your subject. Your wish is my command. Amen!*

> "We know that God is everywhere; but certainly we feel His presence most when His works are on the grandest scale spread before us…"
> —Charlotte Brontë, *Jane Eyre*

INTERACT: God's credentials include the creation of the heavens; the natural order that springs from the Earth; and living, breathing, functioning humans (Isaiah 42:5). How do these credentials give you comfort and elicit trust in Him? (Hint: Isaiah 42:6):

_____
_____
_____
_____

Research a few examples of microevolution. Write your findings here.

_____
_____
_____
_____

I believe adaptation (microevolution) is solid evidence for God's hand in creation, because:

_____
_____
_____
_____

DAY 30

INTELLIGENT DESIGN

> "God saw all that he had made, and it was very good…"
> —Genesis 1:31a

In contrast to Darwinian evolution, a movement called Intelligent Design teaches that "certain features of the universe and of living things are best explained by an intelligent cause rather than an undirected process such as natural selection."*

An ID principle called 'irreducible complexity' explains that some biological systems, like the eye, cannot be formed by successive modifications, as evolution requires. Each component must be present and fully developed before the eye can see. Intelligent Design denies that a working human eye could be the product of evolution.

A simple example is the mouse trap. It will only catch mice once all parts are present, in workable condition and assembled properly. You need a base; a spring; a catch that releases the spring; a metal hammer that kills the mouse; and a metal bar that holds the hammer back. If anything is amiss, the mice run wild.

It's appalling how venomous many evolutionary scientific types are toward Intelligent Design. You would think a reasoned and polite discussion could ensue about the not–so–preposterous idea that things that exist had an intelligent designer.

Why do so many scientists argue rabidly against Intelligent Design? First, if ID is true, many scientists will be forced to admit they are utterly, preposterously wrong about evolution. How embarrassing!

Second, what could you say to that Intelligent Designer? How could you explain rejecting the reasonable notion that stuff came into existence by the loving act of a benevolent Creator, once He is standing in judgment of you?

Another explanation for the vitriolic, venomous opposition to Intelligent Design comes from William Provine, a science historian at Cornell University. "The most basic problem is that [ID is] utterly boring," he says. "Everything that's complicated or interesting about biology has a very simple explanation: Intelligent Design did it." Somehow, twiddling your thumbs for millions of years, waiting for evolution to do its business, is biologically scintillating?

Many critics of intelligent design argue that ID is not science due to its proponents' alleged religious motives, beliefs, and affiliations. Note the lack of scientific refutation in this argument. Interestingly, evolution has its own religious motives, beliefs and affiliations.

A Christian and an evolutionist rode a train from New York to Toronto together. The second fellow remarked how nicely someone had arranged white rocks on a hillside, saying, "WELCOME TO CANADA." When the Christian asked why the skeptic was certain human hands had arranged the rocks, the evolutionist scoffed at the idea that the rocks could roll into that message unassisted. He missed the irony of his contradictory evolutionary beliefs.

WHAT'S THE POINT?: *Divine creation displays design, order and purpose. This suggests an intelligent mind behind the whole universe, a terrifying thought to all who refuse allegiance and loyalty to this Supreme Being.*

> When people become violently angry because you suggest things are made by someone, you can't help but doubt secular human "wisdom."

PRAYER: *Almighty God, creator of heaven and earth, show me how to be a purveyor of Your creativity to those around me. Amen!*

INTERACT: If God looked at the six days of creation and pronounced it "very good" by His elevated standards (Genesis 1:31), what should we think of His handicraft?

_____

_____

_____

_____

Jot a few notes about evolution's "religious motives, beliefs, and affiliations."

_____

_____

_____

_____

_____

* http://www.intelligentdesignnetwork.org/

Go to a search engine and research "Intelligent Design." You will find many sites, both pro–ID and pro–evolution.

Additional resources about origins: (http://www.darwins-theory-of-evolution.com).

DAY 31

RAGS TO RATS

> "From this time many of his disciples turned back and no longer followed him. ⁶⁷'You do not want to leave too, do you?' Jesus asked the Twelve. ⁶⁸Simon Peter answered him, 'Lord, to whom shall we go? You have the words of eternal life. ⁶⁹We have come to believe and to know that you are the Holy One of God.'"
> —John 6:66–69

Evolutionists object to the need for faith to believe in biblical creation. Yet faith is required in any theory of origins. It comes down to "Whose explanation will you believe? The Bible, modern science, your own infallibility, or...?"

A fundamental principle of the scientific method is what we call "trial and error." There is nothing wrong with it. But it means there will be many, many potholes on the road to truth. Historically, science has worked hard to correct its errors, which have been many (right, Flat Earthers?).

For example, science once theorized that rags and other filth left lying around turned into rats. There was a strong correlation between rags and rats. Eventually, science got it right. Those rags left lying around *attracted* rats but did not actually *become* rats.

The track record for being right strongly favors the Bible's version of truth. It's burdensome to drum up enough faith to swallow evolution. The Bible has a much stronger track record than trial and error science.

The chances of the trillion evolutionary processes needed to happen in perfect order are too remote to take evolution seriously.

For millions, believing that Darwin's theory of evolution presents the best explanation for origins takes more faith than believing in a divine Creator.*

There's no escaping the need for faith: Either you trust the Bible or you trust Darwin. Faith is indispensable for either theory.

WHAT'S THE POINT?: *Which explanation for origins will you trust? The only way to dispense with the need for faith is to believe nothing about everything. And that's a tall order, indeed!*

PRAYER: *Lord God of Heaven and Earth, I choose to trust You and to follow wherever You lead me. Amen!*

INTERACT: In first–century Judaism, blasphemy was punishable by death. How radical do you think Peter's words are in John 6:69?

_____
_____
_____
_____

If a person rejects faith in God, how should Peter's words, "Lord, to whom shall we go? You have the words of eternal life" (John 6:68) affect that decision?

_____
_____
_____
_____

*Geisler, Norman L. & Frank Turek, *I Don't Have Enough Faith to Be an Atheist*, Wheaton: Crossway Books, 2004

DAY 32
BLESS GOD, BLESS YOU

> "...Great and marvelous are your deeds, Lord God Almighty. Just and true are your ways, King of the nations. ⁴Who will not fear you, Lord, and bring glory to your name? For you alone are holy. All nations will come and worship before you, for your righteous acts have been revealed."
> —Revelation 15:3b–4

Why did God go to all the trouble of creating so lavishly? It's not because mankind has anything that God needs. But this completeness of God found in the Trinity doesn't mean He has no wants or desires.

George Barna explains in *Think Like Jesus* why God created the world and everything in it. "The mountains, the seas, animals—everything He created before humankind fulfills His will and brings Him pleasure. But it is humans alone who can grasp the incredible sophistication and beauty of the universe and give God meaningful and heartfelt respect, praise, and worship as a result of His handiwork."

God wants love, worship, admiration, and praise from His creation. He gets joy and pleasure from your worship, but the primary beneficiary of all this attention you give to God is—*you*. Creation itself is a song of never–ending praise to God. He has *created* to bless and be blessed. Your worship of God blesses and changes you as nothing else can.

WHAT'S THE POINT?: *God doesn't need our praise and worship. But He surely does enjoy it. The blessings we receive from blessing God are a sign of His wonderful grace.*

Is God on an ego trip? What's with all this attention He seems to crave? Are we scratching an itch that God can't reach by Himself?

PRAYER: *Blessed Lord, as I offer sincere and willing praise to You, I find myself blessed and built up. Thank You for Your undeserved, unearned blessings of grace. Amen!*

INTERACT: How did John use the word "fear" in Revelation 15:4?

_____

_____

_____

_____

How is "fear of the Lord" a good thing?

_____

_____

_____

_____

How do praise and worship bring pleasure to God?

_____

_____

_____

_____

My praise and worship of God have changed ME in this way:

_____

_____

_____

_____

DAY 33
BECAUSE HE CAN

> "[The Spirit of the Lord has anointed me] to proclaim the year of the LORD's favor and the day of vengeance of our God, to comfort all who mourn, ³and provide for those who grieve in Zion—to bestow on them a crown of beauty instead of ashes, the oil of joy instead of mourning, and a garment of praise instead of a spirit of despair. They will be called oaks of righteousness, a planting of the LORD for the display of his splendor." —Isaiah 61:2–3

When Jesus fed the five thousand (Matthew, chapter 14), why did He make so much that it took twelve large baskets to collect the leftovers? It's simple. Jesus was having so much fun He didn't want to stop.

A similar sentiment might explain why natural creation is resplendent with color, variety, beauty, and over-abundance. God's desire for creative expression is sometimes mimicked by human creativity. A world traveler explained what she found in the far, hidden recesses of the Taj Mahal in India. Out front is a magnificent display of intricate craftsmanship and awe–inspiring detail. When she got a glimpse of the part that few ever see, she was amazed to discover the same level of skill and attention to detail. The pleasure and satisfaction of creating are rewards in themselves.

One of the reasons God created is simply, "Because He could!" He had the capacity plus the desire; He was willing and able. So, He created. And He derived pleasure from making it the biggest, most beautiful, most awe–inspiring, most prolific, beyond imagining.

For example, why are there more than 8.7 million animal species on earth? Wouldn't a million be enough? Why 8.7 million? It's because

God enjoys both creating and giving us the ability to create.

Why are there an infinite number of shapes in snowflakes—and never one repeated? Just because God can, and He derives pleasure from such prolific creation.

There are 8 billion people on this planet, and about that many have been born and died since Adam. And not one exact duplicate! God loves to create—and it shows!

WHAT'S THE POINT?: *God is really, really good at creating. And He put within you and me a talent and love for creating too. It's His image in us, peeking around the curtain.*

> **"God must have made some parts of creation for sheer fun—how else would you account for the kangaroo?"**
> —G. K. Chesterton

PRAYER: *God, thank You for instilling within me the ability and interest to create. May others see You when they look at me. Amen!*

INTERACT: What comes to mind when you read Isaiah's words "crown of beauty," "ashes," "oil of joy," and "spirit of despair" (61:2–3)?

_____

_____

_____

_____

Here's what I will do to be an "oak of righteousness, a planting of the Lord for the display of His splendor:"

_____

_____

_____

_____

Describe the pleasure and satisfaction you experience in some act of creating:

_____
_____
_____
_____

DAY 34

THIRD ROCK FROM THE SUN

> "'For I know the plans I have for you,' declares the LORD, 'plans to prosper you and not to harm you, plans to give you hope and a future.'"
> —Jeremiah 29:11

The Bible presents creation as a process with a great cosmic purpose. Evolution embraces completely haphazard chance through measureless time periods. But if creation really does show purpose—having been intentionally formed by a loving, all-powerful Supreme Being—then everyone will have to bow to this Creator's moral standard, or submit to His just judgment.

Speaking of moral standards, Ray Comfort, author, speaker and CEO of Living Waters Ministry, says when he talks to an avowed atheist, he asks, "Can you be brutally honest with me?" When he says that he can, Comfort responds, "This has little to do with the existence of God and everything to do with you having sex with your gorgeous girlfriend. Am I right?" And, in almost every case, the reaction is an admission that his problem isn't with God's existence but His moral demands.*

Science itself has unintentionally provided many signs of intelligence and purpose in creation. Here are a few.

- If gravity changed by even a small amount, all the planets in our solar system would be realigned, and life as we know it here on Earth would be impossible.
- If the speed of light (186,000 miles per second, 5.88 trillion miles per year) was slightly slower or faster, the stars surrounding our Earth (including the sun) would be either too dim or too bright for life as we know it.

- If Earth had a different axial tilt, temperatures would be so different that most of Earth's flora and fauna could not exist here. The yearly fluctuation between 22.1– and 24.5–degrees angle brings huge climatic extremes, from Death Valley, California (world record +130°) to Vostok, Antarctica (world record –128.6°)!
- If the depth of Earth's crust was slightly different, it would change the oxygen content, and life on this terrestrial ball would be snuffed out.
- Then there are conditions like earthquake frequency, Earth's magnetic field, rotation cycles of the Earth, and the relationship of Earth's and the moon's gravitational fields, all of which would leave the third rock from the sun with a very different, hostile environment, unfit for human habitation.

Every facet of life has been delicately balanced by an all–knowing, all–powerful, beneficent Creator. This precise design could not happen randomly, by chance, with no all–knowing, all–powerful Creator–Sustainer to guide it.

Psalm 8 says humankind is assigned the task of ruling over God's creation. Jesus's followers should cherish and protect the environment as caretakers in God's system. Believers should be some of the most dedicated environmentalists (I do *not* mean Earth worshipers).

WHAT'S THE POINT?: *The universe is a precisely tuned mega–system. Planet Earth shows the fingerprints of God everywhere you look.*

> **God's plans for you fit exactly within the framework of His precise and majestic creation.**

PRAYER: *Dear Creator God, Earth may be insignificant in the vastness of the universe, but it suits Your crowning achievement, mankind, exactly. Thank You, Amen!*

INTERACT: Though the words of Jeremiah 29:11 were spoken primarily to Jewish people headed for captivity in Babylon, how can they relate to you today?

_____
_____
_____
_____

God's plans for me have led to prosperity, hope, and a promising future that includes:

_____
_____
_____
_____

As one of God's creation managers, I want to protect the environment while making good use of Earth's abundant resources by:

_____
_____
_____
_____

* From *Christian Post* news website, July 27, 2023

How to reach a prodigal son or daughter, www.christianpost.com

DAY 35

SO WHAT? NOW WHAT?

> "The wrath of God is being revealed from heaven against all the godlessness and wickedness of people, who suppress the truth by their wickedness, [19]since what may be known about God is plain to them, because God has made it plain to them. [20]For since the creation of the world God's invisible qualities—his eternal power and divine nature—have been clearly seen, being understood from what has been made, so that people are without excuse."
> —Romans 1:18–20

Dr. Haddon Robinson's "Big Idea" concept teaches preaching students to state the nucleus of their sermons in one simple statement. And the message should offer an application for daily life. I had a colleague who said at the end of most sermons, "So what? Now what?" What will you do with what you've just learned?

Correspondingly, what do creation and the character of God offer that you can put to use in the everyday world you live in? Creation shows purpose, order, imagination, beauty, dependability, intelligence, functionality... in other words, it all works.

These qualities are facets of God's divine character and show up naturally in what He has created. The result is your appreciation of, and love for God are enhanced when you see the perfection of His character, as shown in Scripture, in nature and through His image in us.

Then you can face daily challenges, decisions, and even tragedies, with those traits of God's nature showing through every crack and flaw in your surface. No wonder God allows Christians to struggle with the same troubles nonbelievers face. You can survive and thrive and demonstrate success.

Those struggles are opportunities for what President George H.W. Bush called "a thousand points of light." The illumination of God's image shines through mankind's everyday difficulties to illuminate a loving, patient, resourceful God ready to lift His downfallen people to new heights of worship, joy, and usefulness.

WHAT'S THE POINT?: *The qualities of God's nature that He has built into us make it possible to rise above the mundane plane of routine and reflect His glory to a dark, fallen world.*

So what? Now what? How will you apply the biblical truths in these readings to your daily life?

PRAYER: *Lord God, please help me use the stuff I am made of to succeed in this less–than–perfect world. Your nature in me provides all I need to survive and thrive. Amen!*

INTERACT: Here is something I have learned about God which I hope to make plain to others:

_____
_____
_____
_____

One practical application about God's creation that has blessed me is:

_____
_____
_____

What is one principle, from what you have learned so far in this book, that you will apply in your own life?

_____
_____
_____

DAY 36

I AM A FRIEND OF GOD!

> "And the scripture was fulfilled that says, 'Abraham believed God, and it was credited to him as righteousness,' and he was called God's friend." —James 2:23

God had at least two purposes for creating the universe where we live. First, He satisfied His great creative genius, making astonishing, magnificent things out of nothing.

Second, God put in place the apparatus for rich, satisfying relationships with His favorite creation, you. In Genesis, chapter 3, He was enjoying daily fellowship with Adam and Eve "in the cool of the evening," like hanging out after work. Then the humans chose to rebel and make an end–run around God. The fellowship they enjoyed was truncated, cut off mid–sentence.

God did not accept the new status quo, however. He formulated a plan B to reconnect with humanity in warm, loving relationships. God the Son became the tiny baby Jesus and lived the entirety of the human experience. Then He died to pay the price for mankind's sin, and rose from death to institute eternal life for all who trust Him as Savior.

So, what is your response to God's initiative? How will you RSVP to His invitation? Will you make selfish choices, refusing to submit to Jesus? Will you stay the rebellious course with Adam and Eve? Or will you become a Jesus follower? It is the central decision in life.

> **Mr. Rogers wants to be your neighbor. Jesus Christ wants to be your friend.**

For all who aspire to be like Jesus, building and deepening your relationship with God will be one of life's highest priorities—and pleasures. When your relationships with God and each other are a high priority, it will change the way you view the world. Selfish agendas will be reordered and other people and their welfare will increase in importance. The time and effort you dedicate to God will motivate everything else.

When we were raising our daughters, we wanted to be their friends. But sometimes the job of teaching them how to live their lives was a higher priority than friendship. It is the same with God. His friendship with you will never overpower His purpose of growing you into His kind of person, the one He saw in His mind's eye when He created you.

WHAT'S THE POINT?: *God achieved two things by creating: a marvelous–beyond–words universe of awe–inspiring beauty and immensity; and a way to restore His intimate relationship with humanity. How will you respond?*

What a great musical exclamation point you will find on YouTube.com: "Friend of God" by Israel Houghton (HQ w/lyrics)

PRAYER: *Dear Lord Jesus, I accept Your invitation to a close, loving friendship. Please guide me as I become a Jesus follower. Amen!*

INTERACT: Faith in God qualifies a believer to be called "God's friend" (James 2:23). Lord, help me, Your friend, with my faith in this way:

_____

_____

_____

_____

How does God connect with you in a warm, loving relationship?

_____

_____

_____

How has James 2:23 been fulfilled?
_____
_____
_____
_____

Write out your response to God's RSVP to build a friendship with Him:
_____
_____
_____
_____

DAY 37

I PLEDGE ALLEGIANCE…

> "The [governing council] called the apostles in and had them flogged. Then they ordered them not to speak in the name of Jesus, and let them go. ⁴¹The apostles left the Sanhedrin, rejoicing because they had been counted worthy of suffering disgrace for the Name. ⁴²Day after day, in the temple courts and from house to house, they never stopped teaching and proclaiming the good news that Jesus is the Messiah."
> —Acts 5:40–42

Synonyms of the word *devoted* include keen, enthusiastic, dedicated, faithful, loyal, devout, and fervent. These terms may help us understand better what being devoted to something or someone involves. Devoted people often do radical, almost irrational things in response to their enthusiasm.

The late John McCain (the Arizona Senator for thirty-one years) spent over five years as a prisoner in North Vietnam. After years of solitary confinement, their jailers put the POWs in large cells holding thirty to forty men. They also started delivering packages and letters from home.

In McCain's cell was a Navy officer, Mike Christian. He gathered bits and pieces of red and white cloth from various packages. Using a piece of bamboo he fashioned into a needle, Mike sewed a US flag inside his blue prison shirt.

Every night, Mike would hang his shirt–flag on the wall, and they would say the pledge of allegiance. This went on for some time until one of the guards caught them reciting the pledge. They ripped the flag off the wall and dragged Mike out. He was beaten for hours, then thrown back into the cell.

"Later that night, as we were settling down to sleep on our concrete beds," McCain recalled, "I looked over to where the guards had thrown Mike. There, under the solitary lightbulb, I saw him, still bloody, face swollen beyond recognition. He was gathering bits and pieces of cloth together, sewing a new American flag" (McCain told this story when addressing the Republican National Convention in 1988).

Mike Christian loved America, and his devotion led to almost insane bravery, starting to make another American flag.

If a man can be that devoted to his country, can we be just as keen, enthusiastic, dedicated, ardent, faithful, loyal, devout, and fervent about God our Creator? And if we *do* love God that much, what changes might we make in our progress toward becoming like Jesus?

WHAT'S THE POINT?: *Our devotion, loyalty and enthusiasm for Jesus can only move us to worship. Our gratitude will take us to new heights of praise, dedication and joyful service.*

> **Make me a blessing...out of my life may Jesus shine... Make me a blessing to someone today.***

PRAYER: *Dear God of Wonders Beyond our Galaxy, show me how to turn my devotion to You into acts of love and service that make a difference in the lives of individuals. Amen!*

INTERACT: The Jewish council ordered the apostles not to talk about Jesus anymore (Acts 5:40). What do you make of their disobedience?

_____
_____
_____
_____

I have seen radical, almost irrational things done in the name of Jesus. Here's a sample:

_____

_____

_____

_____

How do you plan to be a blessing to someone today, to let Jesus shine out of your life?

_____

_____

_____

_____

*"Make Me a Blessing" lyrics by Ira Bishop Wilson, music by George S. Shuler.

4
LIFE'S FIVE VALUES*

(Days 38–52)

To complement your experience in Chapter Four, go to www.YouTube.com and watch 4HIM – "The Basics of Life"

---

* 1) Love God.

2) Love others (personal family, church family, strangers).

3) Love yourself.

4) Prioritize your work.

5) Do good works in Jesus's name.

DAY 38
WRITE YOUR OWN EPITAPH

"For I [Paul] am already being poured out like a drink offering, and the time for my departure is near. [7] I have fought the good fight, I have finished the race, I have kept the faith. [8] Now there is in store for me the crown of righteousness, which the Lord, the righteous Judge, will award to me on that day—and not only to me, but also to all who have longed for his appearing."
—2 Timothy 4:6–8

Our priorities mirror our values. Living on purpose sounds easier than it is. One way to keep *the main thing* the main thing (as John Maxwell has coined it) is to ask yourself what they might chisel on your tombstone.

In his book *The Grand Essentials*, Ben Patterson explains his theory about old age. When life has boiled you down, when the body fails and wrinkles steal your beauty and arteries harden, what is left is your pure essence. He provides two examples.

Patterson identifies 'Exhibit A' in his family. It was an uncle who spent his life making money. Then, he spent his old age slobbering, slavering, and babbling about his wealth. When life carved him down to his core, what was left was simple greed he had perfected over a lifetime.

Exhibit B' was Grandma Edna. When she died in her mid-eighties, she had already had dementia for a while. What did this lady talk about? "The best example I can think of," Patterson explains, "was when we asked her to pray before dinner. She would reach out and hold the hands of those sitting beside her, a broad, beatific smile would spread across her face, her dim eyes would fill with tears as she looked up to heaven, and her chin would quiver as she poured out her love to Jesus." Love. That was Edna in a word.

She loved Jesus and she loved people. She could not remember their names, nor could she keep her hands from lovingly patting her family whenever they got within reach. When life whittled her down to her bare essence, all there was left was love for God and for people.

What will you babble about when what's left is the core of your lifetime? Life's five values reflect your priorities. Throughout history people have pondered their priorities. A man asked Jesus that very question. The things that matter most to you right now, today, will show up when you are distilled to the essence of who you became throughout life. That's what you'll babble about when you're old.

LIFE'S FIVE VALUES*

WHAT'S THE POINT?: *Your true essence will show through every mask or disguise.*

PRAYER: *Blessed Christ, help me take stock of who I am becoming and adjust my priorities accordingly. Amen!*

> "Want to be successful? Change your priorities! To change your life, you need to change your priorities."
> —Mark Twain

INTERACT: Today's Scripture reading contains some of Paul's last words in his earthly life. What would you like your last words to be?

_____
_____
_____
_____

Living on purpose requires me to have a plan from God. That needs to include these specifics:

_____
_____
_____
_____

List your five top priorities in life:

_____
_____
_____
_____

DAY 39
SECTION 3, ROW 1, SEAT 6

> "One of the teachers of the law came and heard them debating. Noticing that Jesus had given them a good answer, he asked him, 'Of all the commandments, which is the most important?' [29] 'The most important one,' answered Jesus,' is this: 'Hear, O Israel: The Lord our God, the Lord is one.[30] Love the Lord your God with all your heart and with all your soul and with all your mind and with all your strength.'"
> —Mark 12:28–30

Remember that ubiquitous sign, "John 3:16" at football games? A great many fans probably think it is a message to a latecomer: "John, we are saving your seat in Section 3, row 1, seat 6." But the Bible verse is actually the greatest love note ever written. This love is a two-way street.

The highest priority in human experience is God, represented by reciprocal love. Your motivation shouldn't be 'duty' or 'obligation' to God; the highest value is to *love* God. That is His plan.

People often struggle to put love for God above other things in life. They think it's their duty to put Him first. God doesn't want a 'duty' relationship. He wants intimate love, friendship, delight, and enjoyment. If you are dutifully serving Him but not finding much love, something's wrong. God is eager to share intimacy with us.

In *The Man in the Mirror*, Pat Morley writes, "To know God is to love Him. A man who understands how deeply God longs for a personal relationship with him will be overwhelmed by how God took the initiative in his life."

Jesus, God the Son, also explained, "If you love me, you will obey what I command" (John 14:15). To demonstrate our love for God is to obey Him, and to obey Him is to love Him.

Morley lists four things that demonstrate our love for God: *Bible study*, *prayer*, *worship*, and *serving*.

Making God our first priority is a conscious, deliberate, intentional decision. We may have to work at developing this into a habit. It begins when we decide to put Him first. Have you decided that?

Many are afraid to put God first because they believe it will short-change their pleasure in life. As if being like Jesus will be a second-rate life. Too many delicious pleasures to give up. Don't listen to that lie of the devil.

WHAT'S THE POINT?: *The first and highest priority to which God calls us is our relationship with Him. And love going both ways is the kingpin of that relationship.*

> **Personal and corporate worship, discipleship, fellowship, and stewardship comprise the four Christian '–ships.'**

PRAYER: *Blessed Savior, my life reveals the priorities I really have. Please develop within me a deep, intimate relationship with You. Amen!*

INTERACT: If you love God with all your heart, soul, mind and strength, what's left?

_____
_____
_____
_____

Love for, and obedience to Jesus are partnered in my life in this way:

_____
_____
_____
_____

I feel a duty toward God but not that much love. I think I can develop more love by doing this:

_____

_____

_____

_____

LIFE'S FIVE VALUES*

DAY 40
TWELVE INCHES TOO HIGH

> "[Jesus said] 'Love the Lord your God with all your heart and with all your soul and with all your mind and with all your strength.' ³¹The second is this: 'Love your neighbor as yourself.' There is no commandment greater than these."
> ³²"'Well said, teacher,' the man replied. 'You are right in saying that God is one and there is no other but him. ³³ To love him with all your heart, with all your understanding and with all your strength, and to love your neighbor as yourself is more important than all burnt offerings and sacrifices.'"
> —Mark 12:30–33

Loving God is the first and highest value you can have. The result of loving God is loving His people. The two go hand–in–glove. If our love for God is genuine, we will love our neighbors (sometimes it may take a little time). And to do justice to neighbor–love, we need the transformation God offers to change our lives from self–centered to God–centric.

That last verse in today's Scripture says, "To love him with all your heart...and to love your neighbor as yourself is more important than any burnt offerings and sacrifices."

Perhaps you have been driven by the *rituals* of faith, trying to satisfy God with the modern equivalent of burnt offerings and sacrifices. Under those circumstances, loving your neighbor will be a tiresome and inconvenient chore, not an extension of your love relationship with God.

Since the beginning of time, humankind has tended toward the trappings of a relationship with God instead of the real McCoy. Isaiah was inspired by the Holy Spirit to write, "The Lord says: 'These people come near to me with their mouth and honor me with their lips, but their hearts are far from me. Their worship of me is based on merely human rules they have been taught'" (Isaiah 29:13). Anyone who puts mere head knowledge before a heart-bond has their faith about twelve inches too high, in their head, not their heart.

WHAT'S THE POINT?: *God does not care about the mindless words we speak, the rote recitations of our minds, or the sullen duties we have discharged. He cares about love from the heart.*

> "When it comes time for God to judge us, he will not ask, 'How many good things have you done in your life?' Rather he will ask, 'How much love did you put into what you did?'" —Mother Teresa

PRAYER: *Father God, please expose the mindless things I do that are not real worship. Cultivate in me a love for You and Your people. Amen!*

INTERACT: What would have to change for you to "love your neighbor as you love yourself"?

_____

_____

_____

_____

I have the "burnt offerings and sacrifices" to God down pat. But to keep the spirit of His Word, I need to elevate love above rituals. My first step should be:

_____

_____

_____

_____

How have you come near to God with your lips, while your heart has been distant and disengaged?

_____

_____

_____

_____

DAY 41
LIFE TO THE MAX!

> "I am the gate [of the sheep pen]; whoever enters through me will be saved. They will come in and go out, and find pasture. ¹⁰The thief comes only to steal and kill and destroy; I have come that they may have life, and have it to the full."
> —John 10:9–10

Priority one in life is loving God, never letting anything else come before Him. In fact, anything you prioritize ahead of God is an idol. Idolatry in the twenty-first century, you ask? You bet. I've met people who might be willing to lay down their very lives if their football team could just win a Super Bowl!

One objection to putting God first is that the rest of your life might suffer. No more fun, no more pleasure, no more excitement. That doesn't dovetail with Jesus's words, "I have come to give you abundant life to the max!"

Putting God first never short-changes anything else. In fact, a life in harmony with Jesus maximizes true satisfaction. You might sometimes think, "If I put God first, my family (or my career or hobby) will suffer!" Nothing could be further from the truth.

When you put Him first in your life, as the highest priority, He blesses all those other things—family, work, personal life—like never before (Matthew 6:33).

It's kind of like putting an Energizer battery into a flashlight with the bump pointed the wrong way. The device simply will not work! But when you get the batteries in with the little bump on the correct end, suddenly, the light comes on!

Putting God first makes everything else in life better! God takes the guilt out of life and allows you more satisfaction. Want more success? Careers guided by God's standards are more successful. Want more satisfaction? The King of kings is also the King of satisfaction (Ecclesiastes 2:24). Want to live life on purpose? That's exactly what God wants for you too. Want better–adjusted, happier kids? The Bible is the textbook for raising them.

You might feel that making God your first priority is a sacrifice. In reality, all you give up is guilt, anger, fear, greed, all those negatives caused by Satan. He is behind our rejection of God as priority one. Don't believe his lie that life will be dull and uninteresting if you follow Jesus.

WHAT'S THE POINT?: *There's no success or satisfaction in life as great as finding yourself right where God wants you to be.*

PRAYER: *Dear Jesus, please fill my life with success, satisfaction and living on purpose, when I put You on the throne of my heart. Amen!*

> "That 'something' you seek is God's best life for you...It is everything good and right for you and your future... it means being the best you that you can possibly be."
> —Wintley Phipps, *Your Best Destiny*

INTERACT: Jesus used many agricultural figures of speech, like a 'sheep pen' in today's reading. What would be a good modern illustration of the abundant life Jesus offers?

_____

_____

_____

_____

I once got a flashlight battery in, wrong end too. It resulted in:

_____

_____

_____

_____

How have you thought that putting God first might create a "power outage" in life?

LIFE'S FIVE VALUES*

DAY 42
HEY, THAT WAS DAD!

> "God sets the lonely in families... "
> —Psalm 68:6a
> "If anyone does not provide for his relatives, and especially for his immediate family, he has denied the faith and is worse than an unbeliever."
> —1 Timothy 5:8

After valuing God first, other people in your life should rank second in priority. Someone coined the old proverb, "J•O•Y spells 'Jesus, Others, and You.'" Many people find that the *best* (and yes, the *worst*) times in life center on family. When we were raising teenage girls, we had some difficult times. Today, those girls have teenagers of their own. Our greatest joys—and sorrows—come from our kids and their kids.

It's easy to get off–balance in this realm. Some people give their family members little time, attention, or guidance. I have known pastors who used the excuse of ministering to justify neglecting their own families. Other people smother their family members, unintentionally pushing them away.

One reason Jesus spent the earlier years of His life in obscurity, may have been His love and responsibility to His earthly family. Many historians doubt that Joseph survived until Jesus's life of ministry. As the firstborn son, Jesus would have had the primary duty to care for His earthly family. Scripture teaches that valuing your family is second only to valuing God. Nothing else in life comes ahead of family. This priority includes having fun and making lifelong memories.

An East Coast family planned a West Coast vacation, but Dad could not leave on time. So, with the family driving through the western desert without him, he made secret arrangements to meet them there. When the family's station wagon whizzed past the hitchhiker, one of the children shouted, "I think that was Dad!" The roadside reunion was full of fun, and made lifelong memories. When asked why he would do such a crazy thing, he explained, "After I die, I want my kids to say, 'Dad sure was fun, wasn't he?'"

> "God first, family second, career third."
> —Mary Kay Ash
>
> "Next to God, family is the best thing."
> —April Floyd

WHAT'S THE POINT?: *Family life is a great place to influence others toward faith in Jesus. Use your time wisely, and enjoy the journey.*

PRAYER: *Blessed Father, please show me how to model my relationships with my family members after Your relationship with me. Amen!*

INTERACT: Who do you know that's lonely? How could you be available for God to put a lonely person in your family? (today's Scripture):

_____
_____
_____
_____

Has family influence made contributions to your faith? If so, explain how it helped:

_____
_____
_____
_____

I find it challenging to keep proper order in my God–first and family–second priorities. ❏ Yes ❏ No

LIFE'S FIVE VALUES*

DAY 43
A SPIRIT OF UNIVERSITY

> "Therefore, as we have opportunity, let us do good to all people, especially to those who belong to the family of believers."
> —Galatians 6:10

As God becomes the pinnacle of your life, you also recognize the elevated value of loving others. This includes your church family.

A woman named Sheila once told my wife that she felt closer to her church family, in many ways, than she did to her blood relatives. When you share heart and soul beliefs with your church family, it can elevate your life in ways that even blood relatives may not.

When we make church family members a priority, we want to be with them, we want to grow and help them grow, we want to worship and learn and be together. Call it "body life." It is God's plan for Jesus followers to promote the essential value of a spiritual family.

Church is not simply where you meet your friends. It's not a building. Church is one track you ride to influence the world around you. Church is who you are. The Church is a vehicle through which the person of Jesus Christ transforms communities and social systems. Don't just go to church; BE the church in the world, Christ's body on Earth.

This process represents a logical progression from personal intimacy with Jesus to spiritual formation within the biological family, to connection with the wider community of people journeying together toward the goal of being like Jesus.

How many times have you used the word *university* without knowing its origin? It literally represents "**UNi**ty in di**VERSITY**." That may be an even better description of the body of Jesus Christ. First Corinthians, chapter 12, explains this unity in diversity beautifully.

It all fits within the first of the values examined in Chapter Four of *Being Like Jesus* —your priorities!

> There is a family besides the one whose DNA you share. Ideally, you love them beyond words and would do anything for them. And they for you.

WHAT'S THE POINT?: *Being part of God's church makes life better. The life-giving intimacy of shared Christian beliefs increases the likelihood of surviving and thriving in a cold, dark, secular world spinning out of control without Jesus.*

PRAYER: *Dear Christ, guide me to a loving, nurturing family of believers, so I can both give and receive strength, joy and purpose. Amen!*

INTERACT: Paul explained that doing good for fellow believers is crucial (Galatians 6:10). I am making that a priority by:

_____
_____
_____
_____

How have Church family members elevated your life of faith?

_____
_____
_____
_____

Where are you on the continuum from salvation to spiritual growth and maturity in the Christian community?

_____
_____
_____
_____

LIFE'S FIVE VALUES*

UN**ity* in diVERSITY*** has blessed my Christian life by:

_____

_____

_____

_____

DAY 44

ANGELS IN THE GUEST ROOM

> "Keep on loving one another as brothers and sisters. ² Do not forget to show hospitality to strangers, for by so doing some people have shown hospitality to angels without knowing it."
> —Hebrews 13:1–2

Life's second value also focuses on love for strangers. Openness to strangers might be more challenging in the twenty-first century than it was in the first. Phones are programmed to scream "Scam Likely" when you get calls from questionable sources. You also may shy away from opening yourself to random people you do not know.

If you are becoming like Jesus, however, it is a risk you must consider taking, with safeguards. Jesus explained, in Matthew, chapter 25, that when you feed the hungry, give drink to the thirsty, invite strangers into your life, clothe the destitute, and visit the lonely, you are actually doing acts of kindness for the proxies of Jesus. It also makes you a "little Jesus" to the needy.

When our daughters were young, we showed kindness to a drifter named Bob, who passed through our small Ohio city. He did laundry at our house, ate a meal with us, and listened to our little girls' chatter. They talked about Bob for weeks after he moved on, and nothing dangerous happened because of our generosity. It could have, and we would never have forgiven ourselves. Yet God was watching out.

From the beginning, God instructed His people to be kind to strangers from around the world or across the street. We might not share our bank account numbers or passwords, but there are things we can do to serve them.

God wants you to value strangers. Their lives and experiences can enrich you, and help you understand the world better. Friendships have been known to develop, bridging cultural divides, language barriers, state lines, even back fences.

American churches have sponsored asylum seekers from dictatorial regimes or the persecuted from totalitarian societies. They have led some to faith in Jesus. Kindness to strangers can open doors to influence them toward faith in God. Even strangers you will never know very well can be influenced by kindness and help.

Showing the love of Jesus to strangers is an extension of loving Jesus. Even a donation to the local rescue mission or Voice of the Martyrs can show Christ's love. It is part of the God–first priority.

WHAT'S THE POINT?: *Be a "little Jesus" to those in great need. It is part of being like Jesus.*

> **Be kind to a stranger. You might change a life—maybe your own.**

PRAYER: *Lord Jesus, every time I thank You for Your blessings, remind me to look for ways to bless strangers. Amen!*

INTERACT: What strangers in your past might have been angels of which you were unaware? Why do you say that?

_____

_____

_____

_____

I would like to be a "little Jesus" to others by:

_____

_____

_____

_____

Explain how kindness to a stranger (maybe you were that stranger?) paid dividends in your life.

LIFE'S FIVE VALUES*

DAY 45

THE CURE FOR SPIRITUAL SCOLIOSIS

> "Come to me, all you who are weary and burdened, and I will give you rest. ²⁹Take my yoke upon you and learn from me, for I am gentle and humble in heart, and you will find rest for your souls."
> —Matthew 11:28–29
>
> "Then, because so many people were coming and going that they did not even have a chance to eat, he said to [the disciples], 'Come with me by yourselves to a quiet place and get some rest.'"
> —Mark 6:31

Life's five values begin with *God*. The second value is *others:* our immediate *families*, then *church* and *strangers*. Surprisingly to some, the third of our life's five virtues embraces loving *ourselves*. ("Love your neighbor as yourself," Luke 10:27.)

Too much embracing of yourself begins to look and smell suspiciously like self-indulgence. Caring for yourself, however, is biblical. Too much needless lifting of heavy burdens, without rest and recovery, begins to give you spiritual scoliosis, curvature of the sacred spine.

Personal physical care enhances every part of your life. It employs three important aspects of life here and now. The first aspect is the rest of the body, mind, and spirit. Kathy and I have been blessed with special restful places where we laid down our burdens for a few days. They include a cottage on Oahu's windward shore; a loaned timeshare on the Florida Gulf coast; a quiet retreat in Lake Geneva, Wisconsin; and a seaside resort on the Greek island of Crete.

A Philippine missionary saw an aged farmer lugging a big load on his shoulder. Someone with an oxcart took pity, giving the poor old fellow a ride. Later he looked back to ensure the elderly gent was okay. To his chagrin, he saw the peasant, riding along, a heavy bundle still bending his back. Some people do not know how to rest and recreate.

Another vital facet of personal physical care is *nutrition*. Society is more cognizant of nutrition today than when I was a boy. Eating the right foods, in sensible quantities, is a smart and godly part of making ourselves a priority in life.

The third protocol for self-care is *exercise*. Some live by the adage, "Pushing 40 is exercise enough!" or, "I get all my exercise jumping to conclusions." Not long after we became aware of Obsessive-Compulsive Disorders, I read about the "jogging disease," where professional men could not seem to stop running. My time in the 101st Airborne cured me of that—stopped me in my tracks!

> "I have never taken any exercise, except sleeping and resting, and I never intend to…Exercise is loathsome."
> —Mark Twain

WHAT'S THE POINT?: *You are God's creation, and He has made you a steward of His handiwork! Take care of yourself.*

PRAYER: *Creator God, please guard me against burning out and rusting out. Remind me to take proper care of myself, between acts of service to Your Kingdom. Amen!*

INTERACT: Explain the yoke Jesus mentioned in Matthew 11:29.

_____

_____

_____

_____

Jesus's comments about rest in today's reading appeal to me in this way:

_____

_____

_____

_____

LIFE'S FIVE VALUES*

I need to enhance my rest, nutrition and/or exercise by doing this:

_____

_____

_____

_____

DAY 46

WILL YOU BE MY NEIGHBOR?

> "On one occasion an expert in the law stood up to test Jesus. 'Teacher,' he asked, 'what must I do to inherit eternal life?' ²⁶'What is written in the Law?' he replied. 'How do you read it?' ²⁷ He answered, 'Love the Lord your God with all your heart and with all your soul and with all your strength and with all your mind'; and, 'Love your neighbor as yourself.'"
> —Luke 10:25–27

Perhaps you have seen that annoying ad as you play a game on your phone or tablet: "Play this game to keep Alzheimer's disease away." One even said, "We guarantee, playing this game will keep you from getting Alzheimer's." But if it doesn't, who will remember to sue, right?

Dementia of various kinds afflicts one in seven Americans over age seventy. Alzheimer's robs loved ones of their personality, yet often leaves a healthy body to flounder in the mental fog for years to come. No one can guarantee mental–emotional health, but there are things you can do to support it.

As part of love value number three (prioritizing ourselves), give regular attention to personal mental–emotional care. Keep personal mental and emotional growth advancing by reading, discovering, nurturing curiosity, learning a new language, tackling an unfamiliar subject, or the like.

Hobbies help keep a sharp edge on mental and emotional balance as compared with the rest of life.

Recognizing, acknowledging, understanding, and discussing your feelings will help safeguard you from feeling all alone. Rev. Fred Rogers, known as Mister Rogers, said that anything human can be mentioned, and anything mentioned can be managed, with the support of others. He asserted that talking about your feelings makes them less overwhelming and scary. Men have a reputation for not talking about feelings. I get that. But why not give it a try.

Developing your relationships helps you deal with negative emotions before they damage you. God created us to live in relationships. It can be a God–ordained safeguard against mental and emotional paralysis.

Love God, yes. Love others, of course. But love yourself too. It says so in the Good Book.

WHAT'S THE POINT?: *The third love value is loving yourself. If Jesus loved you enough to die for you, why would you feel guilty about taking care of one that He loves?*

> "...once you start talking about [experiencing a mental health struggle], you realize that actually you're part of quite a big club."
> —Prince Harry, Duke of Sussex

PRAYER: *Lord God, You created emotions and intellect, just like You created the physical me. Please keep me on the path to mental and emotional health, so I can be all You envision me to be. Amen!*

INTERACT: Jesus told the rich man to love his neighbor as he loved himself (Matthew 19:19). What does Jesus want you to do to love yourself?

_____

_____

_____

_____

I am going to do this to help avoid mental/emotional damage:

_____

_____

_____

_____

Most younger people do not worry about getting dementia. But even a child can be impacted by the dementia of a loved one. I can help care for someone _____ (name please) who has dementia by:

_____

_____

_____

_____

LIFE'S FIVE VALUES*

DAY 47
SOCIAL DISTANCING SYNDROME

> "A new command I give you: Love one another. As I have loved you, so you must love one another. By this everyone will know that you are my disciples, if you love one another."
> —John 13:34–35
>
> "Be devoted to one another in love. Honor one another above yourselves...^{16}Live in harmony with one another. Do not be proud, but be willing to associate with people of low position. Do not be conceited."
> —Romans 12:10, 16

One of the most coherent examples of social distancing, from the nineteenth century, no less, was the forty-year mourning period of Great Britain's Queen Victoria. After Prince Albert, husband of Britain's third female Queen, died in 1861, she never again wore anything but black, and seldom appeared in public, socially distancing herself from the whole British Empire.

The idea of "social distancing" from COVID-19 emerged at the forefront of life. It may or may not have been helpful in stopping a pandemic. But it seemed to threaten a generation already hibernating in darkened rooms, zeroed in on video games and social media. Today, many prefer texting over interacting in person. They may very well chat by text with others in the same room. When I taught Interpersonal Communication in college, a burning question asked by students was, is the Internet improving or impairing communication? And, does social media qualify as effective communication?

Regarding the value of personal social care, we know that God created us to function in relationships, foremost with Him, but also with family, colleagues, and friends. There are people everywhere who have withdrawn from society around them. They may have intentionally eliminated family, neighbors, co–workers, fellow–students and others from personal contact. They are often called "loners." And they may reemerge in violent anti–social attacks against those in their immediate surroundings. Most who isolate themselves from others simply live lonely, disappointed, or otherwise unhappy existences.

To reinforce this God–given relational resource, note things like the length of the relationship, frequency of interaction, positives and negatives from your connection, and so on. You might choose to do a "social tune–up" every year: ask how to improve relationships, make plans to start new friendships, identify people you'd like to know better, spot people who need a friend, confront the need to change, or end a destructive relationship and so on.

Absent statistical support, I suspect there is more common, daily misery from social dysfunction than in any other area.

WHAT'S THE POINT?: *Caring for yourself includes not just mental–emotional, physical and spiritual care. Paying attention to your personal social world is also important.*

> "As much as we complain about other people, there is nothing worse for mental health than a social desert."
> —Charles Montgomery, *Happy City*

PRAYER: *Lord God, please guide me to beneficial relationships. Also, help me find and befriend others for our mutual benefit. Amen!*

INTERACT: One person who knows I am devoted to them in love is:

Here's how they know:

_____

_____

_____

_____

- Someone said that people do not care how much you know ("Knowledge puffs up" 1 Corinthians 8:1) until they know how much you care. When interacting with others, my balance is:

−5	−4	−3	−2	−1	0	−1	−2	−3	−4	−5
Knowledge is everything					Good balance of knowledge & caring {Hint: the best score is zero}					Knowledge is nothing

Since COVID–19 I hesitate to socialize up–close and personal ❏ Yes ❏ No

I am scheduling my "social tune–up" for this date:_____

DAY 48

WORK CAN BE WORSHIP

> A man can do nothing better than to eat and drink and find satisfaction in his work. This too, I see, is from the hand of God.
> —Ecclesiastes 2:24

There are five primary values in the Jesus follower's life. They are: 1, God; 2, Others; 3, Yourself; 4, Work; 5, Good works.

You can build a successful and satisfying life by adhering to God's priorities. For most of us, almost one third of all waking hours will be spent at work. So work is definitely a life value that needs to be aligned in a productive, God–pleasing, position. Priority number four is your employment or calling.

God wants us to enjoy the basics of our existence. While deep meaning and fulfilling engagement help make life worth living, the everyday things like enjoying a bite to eat, resting on the porch swing, and doing a good job for your employer, are also vital to satisfaction in life. Mark Twain even said that the secret of success is making your *vocation* your *vacation*.

King Solomon's conclusion, when he was old and frustrated with life, was Ecclesiastes 2:24.

> "There is nothing better for a man than that he should eat and drink and that he should make his soul enjoy good in his labour. I have also seen that this is from the hand of God." [KJV]

Eating and drinking and enjoying your work is a gift from God's hand. Solomon, a rich, wise, and famous man, spent his lifetime looking for satisfaction in life. He didn't find it in political power as King of Israel. He was not satisfied with fabulous riches. He did not find satisfaction even in having seven hundred wives and a harem that numbered three hundred (not the wisest choice).

Solomon found satisfaction in the simple things: food, drink and his work—his calling. He recognized that this simple gratification was from God Himself.

Joe Gibbs, the famous football coach and NASCAR™ racing team owner, observed that if you enjoy your work, you will consistently do it with excellence, which only adds to the enjoyment. Vincent Van Gogh observed, "Your profession is what you were put on Earth to do—with such passion and such intensity that it becomes spiritual in calling."

WHAT'S THE POINT?: *You'll spend too much of your life working to settle for mere drudgery. God infuses work with a sense of accomplishment and purpose, and takes pleasure in your achievements.*

> **"Success is finding someone who will pay you to do what you would pay to do, if you could afford it."**
> —Sarah Caldwell

PRAYER: *God in heaven, please keep me reminded that, starting with Adam, work was a noble and righteous endeavor. Help me find satisfaction in a job well-done. Amen!*

INTERACT: My work is fulfilling in this way:

_____

_____

_____

How does your work balance these three criteria: 1) a living wage; 2) work enjoyment, and; 3) a chance to live my faith for my co-workers to see?

_____

_____

How might your vocation be your vacation?

Enjoyment in my work has helped me achieve excellence in this way:

LIFE'S FIVE VALUES*

DAY 49

WORSHIP IN A HARDHAT

> "From the fruit of their lips people are filled with good things, and the work of their hands brings them reward."
> —Proverbs 12:14

The alarm clock will ring in thirty minutes. Your dread is so great that you lie awake, waiting for the hated sound. Friends spring out of bed with a smile and eager anticipation for the day. But not you. Someone disabled the excitement setting on your job. It's mindless and mind-numbing, produces high anxiety, or may not stimulate your interest.

Becoming like Jesus gives you a different outlook on work. If your job pays the bills but could be more promising, remember that you probably won't have that job for the rest of your life. Thank God that it meets your immediate needs. Ask Him to guide you toward the long-term plan He has for you. Ask Him to reveal His calling for your life.

As you labor, see the people and tasks around you as missions from God. He has you doing this job for an eternal purpose. He alone knows where your faithfulness and integrity will lead.

Do your very best work, even in a dead-end job. God will bless excellence and multiply your influence in the lives of others. Your faithfulness in an underwhelming job will open new vistas in employment. Trust God for it and keep on plowing. Think of work as an opportunity to glorify God with the gifts, abilities and interests He has given you.

Do not minimize the importance of work. Adam was given meaningful work, even before sin entered the world. Conversely, do not over-emphasize the importance of work. If it becomes your god, it will ultimately break your heart and spirit! One man told his wife, "My job is my god!" When he lost his job, did his god die too?

Do not use work to escape other responsibilities, like intimate time with your children and listening to your spouse.

Bud loved to work as much as anyone I've ever known. He led his family business until age seventy-five, when he had to retire. He told me, "Retirement is the worst job in the world!" Bud was right to love his work. He was a good example of someone who loved to work, almost as much as he loved his family and his Lord. Work was not Bud's god. But it inspired happiness in him. And that's what God intends. If your work is drudgery, there's something wrong!

> "...our daily 'mundane' and 'secular' tasks can glorify God and expand His kingdom... Every task you undertake is a spiritual act of worship."
> —Matt Heerema

WHAT'S THE POINT?: *Consider giving your work to God as an offering from your heart. That would make it sublime worship. Think of it: worship in a hard hat!*

PRAYER: *Dear God, please coach me into loving my work, and finding a new level of excellence. It's a gift of worship to You. Amen!*

INTERACT: What rewards have "the work of your hands" provided you (see today's verse)?

_____

_____

_____

_____

I could make my ho–hum job more rewarding by:

_____

_____

_____

_____

My career could become my god if I do not do this:

_____

_____

_____

_____

One mission from God in my work might be:

_____

_____

_____

_____

DAY 50

GOODY TWO SHOES

> "For we are God's workmanship, created in Christ Jesus to do good works, which God prepared in advance for us to do."
> —Ephesians 2:10

The last of life's five values focuses on good works, the deeds you do that bless those around you. You can actually do good works in every one of the first four priorities, not postponing your good deeds (Ephesians 2:10) until later. They're best when integrated into the whole of life.

Today's short Bible reading identifies three central lessons. First, *you are a sample of God's good workmanship*. He impresses upon His people the importance of creativity, good works, and quality handiwork. You are a prime example of those attributes. You are one of God's good works.

This fact, by itself, is reason enough to have a healthy view of yourself. It is not God's desire that you look down on yourself. We all should look at ourselves as He does—fallen, yes, but also of great value, first of all because He made us. That great song of praise, Psalm 100, asserts, "He made us, and we are His people, sheep in his lush pasture."

The second central lesson from today's Scripture is, *God created you in Christ Jesus for the purpose of doing good works*.

We know that the best of good deeds will not earn His forgiveness. Salvation and good works are only kissing cousins. Redemption is an unearned, undeserved gift of grace. The good works that follow are the result, not the cause, of being right with God. We do good works in His name because we are so grateful for His many blessings.

Third, it might be easy to downplay good works, except that *God went to the cosmic trouble of planning good things, in advance, for you to do.*

He wants to use them to reach lost, unaware and rebellious people with the Good News, the Gospel.

I have always disliked the popular term, "random acts of kindness." God did not plan random good deeds in advance for you to do. He was totally intentional and wants you to execute acts of kindness intentionally.

WHAT'S THE POINT?: *Salvation is by grace alone, followed naturally by actions that bring comfort, guidance and satisfaction to others whom those actions touch.*

You are God's masterpiece. He has designed many good things for you to do. Go and create your own masterpiece.

PRAYER: *Blessed Lord God, reveal to me the good deeds You planned, before the world began, for me to carry out. Then, give me wisdom, strength and eagerness to do them. Amen!*

INTERACT: I can see that God prepared this good work, specifically, in advance for me to accomplish:

_____

_____

_____

_____

How are you an example of God's workmanship?

_____

_____

_____

_____

Here's an example of how God created me in Christ Jesus for the purpose of doing good works:

_____
_____
_____
_____

Since God specifically planned good things for me to do, I will:

_____
_____
_____
_____

LIFE'S FIVE VALUES*

DAY 51

GAIN THE WORLD, FORFEIT THE SOUL

> "[Jesus told His followers] 'You are the light of the world. A town built on a hill cannot be hidden. [15]Neither do people light a lamp and put it under a bowl. Instead they put it on its stand, and it gives light to everyone in the house. [16]In the same way, let your light shine before others, that they may see your good deeds and glorify your Father in heaven.'"
> —Matthew 5:14–16

Most will never understand the heart of God until they see it at work in a Jesus follower. That would qualify you as a "little Jesus," the person who helps others come to faith and begin their lives of service to God and His Kingdom.

Jesus was saying precisely that to the crowd, out on the Galilean hillside. When someone sees your good deeds and glorifies your Father in heaven, that is Being Like Jesus.

In his story, *The Mysterious Island*, Jules Verne told of five men who escaped a Civil War prison by hijacking a hot air balloon. Soon the wind carried them out over the ocean, and they began to descend toward a watery grave. The men were forced to ditch their shoes, overcoats, and even their weapons. The balloon rose, but soon sank again. Reluctantly they tossed their food overboard—better to be high and hungry than drown on a full stomach.

This, too, was only a temporary solution. The five men once more dropped toward the seething ocean. Then one man had an idea: tie together the ropes that held the passenger basket, then cut away the heavy woven container. Immediately the balloon rose sharply. Not a minute too soon, they saw land and jumped into the ocean, swimming to the shore. They were saved.

Things that once were very necessary (like food and weapons) became superfluous when they faced drowning. The very things they thought they could not live without became the burdens that almost killed them.

We ignore the importance of prioritizing, to our peril. Jesus said, "What good will it be for a man if he gains the whole world, yet forfeits his soul? Or what can a man give in exchange for his soul?" (Matthew 16:26).

> "Don't shine so others can see you. Shine so that through you, others can see HIM."
> —C. S. Lewis

WHAT'S THE POINT?: *The five most important values can go a long way towards transforming you into the person God had in mind when He created you (and prepared all those good works).*

PRAYER: *Jesus, a good, accurate evaluation can help me be more like You. Reveal to me how I can become a bigger "little Jesus." Amen!*

INTERACT: How can you do good deeds for others to see, while making sure God gets the glory, not you (Matthew 5:16)?

_____

_____

_____

Possessions I have that may be dragging me down:

_____

_____

_____

LIFE'S FIVE VALUES*

In the interest of elevation in my life, I am reordering my priorities thus:

_____

_____

_____

_____

DAY 52

PRIORITIES, SCHMIORITIES

> "Do not be afraid, little flock, for your Father has been pleased to give you the kingdom. ³³Sell your possessions and give to the poor. Provide purses for yourselves that will not wear out, a treasure in heaven that will never fail, where no thief comes near and no moth destroys. ³⁴For where your treasure is, there your heart will be also."
> —Luke 12:32–34

Time for some soul-searching. We have dedicated the previous two weeks examining the five greatest priorities (according to me) for the person who is interested in Being Like Jesus.

Your priorities reflect your real values. Many say they value one thing, while their life says otherwise. The word 'hypocrite' is harsh, but sometimes it applies. A close, hard look at your priorities may reveal some uncomfortable realities. Or it could reaffirm your faith in action.

Carefully consider the INTERACT section below to evaluate your progress in Life's Five Values.

> "Your priorities aren't what you say they are. They are revealed by how you live."
> —HappyWivesClub.com

WHAT'S THE POINT?: *Someone said, "If you aim at nothing, you're sure to hit it." Clean your gun, choose your target carefully, load good ammunition, and start shooting.*

PRAYER: *Blessed Redeemer, I know my life will be more productive, successful, satisfying and on purpose if I prioritize in a godly way. I need Your help. Amen!*

LIFE'S FIVE VALUES*

INTERACT: What did Jesus mean, "Your Father has been pleased to give you the kingdom"?

_____
_____
_____
_____

What are my priorities? What is my essence? Do they show that I'm becoming more like Jesus? What do they say about me? What am I willing to toss out of my hot air balloon to accomplish my deepest purpose?

_____
_____
_____
_____

Number these five values, based on your real priorities right now:
___ God ___ Others ___ Yourself ___ Work ___ Good works

_____
_____
_____
_____

I want to reprioritize this one area to be transformed into more of a Jesus follower:

_____
_____
_____
_____

What attitudes in your life are dragging you down and limiting your success, satisfaction and purpose?

_____

_____

_____

_____

5
GOD'S GLORY AND PLEASURE

(Days 53–64)
To supplement your experience in Chapter Five, go to
www.YouTube.com and listen to "My Tribute" sung
by Andraé Crouch and The Disciples

DAY 53
SHINE, JESUS, SHINE

"When Jesus spoke again to the people, he said, 'I
am the light of the world. Whoever follows me will never walk in
darkness, but will have the light of life.'"
—John 8:12
"You are the light of the world…"
—Matthew 5:14a

The guru sits cross–legged on the mountaintop in a posture of deep thought. A follower has climbed at great risk and effort, and bows meekly before the wise man. "Why am I here?" he asks humbly.

Most people ask themselves that question. We wonder about our purpose. Evolution says there is no purpose, just random events. Yet, humans long for a life filled with meaning. Is there a greater purpose than just to eat, breathe, sleep, produce, reproduce, take up space, and finally, to fill a plot at the cemetery?

Rick Warren writes, "Without God, life has no purpose, and without purpose, life has no meaning. Without meaning, life has no significance or hope."*

"We were hiking out West," someone recounted, "when I saw a small stone, about the size of a half-dollar. Ordinarily, I would have passed it by. It would have remained there for another thousand years, a mere pebble on the trail.

"But this one instantly caught my eye. Glinting in the sunlight, it reflected the surrounding colors, as though trying to mirror nature. Into my pocket went the rare find. All the way home I thought about where I should display it. I finally placed it in a curio cabinet, next to some jade and carved ivory. I forgot about it for a while.

"Then, one day, I saw it had completely lost its luster, there among the other treasures. It was just a gray chunk of ugly nothing. I was shocked. What had happened to the exquisite prize I had so carefully preserved? Where was the sparkle, the rainbow of vivid colors? Disgusted, I snatched it up and started looking for the trash can in the backyard.

"As I opened the back door, a beam of sunlight struck the stone. As though by magic, it shimmered and glowed again. In an instant the beautiful jewel tones burst into beauty. Had they returned? Or had they always been there, dormant, waiting to wake up? I glanced upward. Sunlight! That was the answer. The dancing rays of sunlight were all my stone needed to erupt."

When lit up by the light of the Son, your life can glow and sparkle and shimmer with beauty. Answering "Why am I here?" becomes easier and much clearer. You are here to reflect the Light of the World to a dark lump of a place, dying for a glimpse of God's purpose.

WHAT'S THE POINT?: *Jesus's followers glorify God and reflect the light of Jesus Christ in a world starved of meaning and purpose.*

PRAYER: *Father of Lights, please shine through me, so I can reflect You toward some sad, gloomy person who needs the Light. Amen!*

> **"Why am I here?"** is more easily answered when your life is being highlighted by the Sonlight of the world.

INTERACT: How could Jesus be right in saying both, "*I* am the light of the world" (John 8:12) and "*You* are the light of the world" (Matthew 5:14)?

_____
_____
_____

Here's how Jesus, the Light, replicates His glow in my life:

_____
_____
_____

Purpose, meaning and hope are connected in my life like this:

_____
_____
_____

* Rick Warren, *The Purpose Driven Life: What on Earth Am I Here for?*

DAY 54

GUTS AND GLORY

> "I consider that our present sufferings are not worth comparing with the glory that will be revealed in us. [19]For the creation waits in eager expectation for the children of God to be revealed. [20]For the creation was subjected to frustration, not by its own choice, but by the will of the one who subjected it, in hope [21]that the creation itself will be liberated from its bondage to decay and brought into the freedom and glory of the children of God."
> —Romans 8:18–21

The stone in yesterday's reading was dull and lifeless without the sunlight. But what was listless under a brooding cloud became a special item of glory and beauty when lit by shafts of solar splendor.

How much like you and me! When we confine ourselves to our own wisdom and intrigues, selfishly refusing to let God lead, life becomes empty, frustrating and devoid of meaning. Only when touched by the glory of God will your inner beauty emerge. In return, trusting God to lead and reflect His glory, you begin to take on fulfillment, a rainbow of color, meaning, and such satisfaction.

Without Him—empty nothingness. With Him, vibrant, pulsating, full–to–overflowing life that displays, for everyone to see, the value and purpose and meaning of human earthly existence.

C.S. Lewis wrote, "We may ignore, but we can nowhere evade the presence of God. The world is crowded with Him. He walks everywhere incognito." It is His people's purpose to reflect His glory and thus remove the label, "incognito" from the Creator and Sustainer of all things.

But first, we must subdue the almighty self, as famous British preacher Charles Spurgeon wrote: "You will never glory in God till first of all God has killed your glorying in yourself."

WHAT'S THE POINT?: *God has a great purpose for each person, a reason for your existence. A fulfilling life depends on living out God's intended purpose, by bringing glory to* Pantakrator,* *Isaac Newton's description of the Supreme Ruler of the universe.*

This must be why we are here: To enjoy, and to reflect, the glory of God.

PRAYER: *Lord, there is no greater satisfaction in human experience than to fulfill our God-given purpose. May You receive glory from my life. Amen!*

INTERACT: How can your present suffering result in God's glory being made visible to others (Romans 8:18)?

_____
_____
_____
_____

When was creation "subjected to frustration"? How will it be liberated from its "bondage to decay"?

_____
_____
_____
_____

Here's how my human 'wisdom and intrigues' have clouded the prism of godly color shining in my life:

_____
_____
_____
_____

My plan to dispel the clouds and let the Son shine through includes:

_____

_____

_____

_____

* *The Principia: Mathematical Principles of Natural Philosophy*, by Sir Issac Newton.

DAY 55

GIVE GOD SOME PLEASURE

> "For he chose us in him before the creation of the world to be holy and blameless in his sight. In love ⁵he predestined us for adoption to sonship through Jesus Christ, in accordance with his pleasure and will— ⁶to the praise of his glorious grace, which he has freely given us in the One he loves."
> —Ephesians 1:4–6

God has a purpose for you. It functions in two realms. The first is here-and-now, the temporal present. The second is God's purpose for your eternity, beyond the reach of time.

Our God-given purpose now, in this life, is to bring glory to God, for a variety of reasons. Glorifying God changes you in many wonderful ways. It also attracts unbelievers to the glory of God by burnishing His reputation through the believer's life. This expands the reach of His magnificent grace to those who have not yet benefited from it.

How are we able to glorify God? Are you ready for this? First, by bringing pleasure to God. Rick Warren (*The Purpose Driven Life*, p. 63) writes, "You exist for [God's] benefit, His glory, His purpose, and His delight." God experienced great enjoyment simply in creating you. Honoring and following Him only increases the great satisfaction God gets from you. Living your life is a source of joy to God, if you honor and glorify Him for everything He has done.

Everything we do that brings pleasure to God is called 'worship.' A new slant on worship, to be sure. This is one vital way we fulfill God's purpose for us—we worship Him, and that gives Him inestimable pleasure.

WHAT'S THE POINT?: *God takes great pleasure in being glorified* *by His crowning creation. It is a never-ending cycle of worship that gives God pleasure, which produces the desire for more worship, which in turn is pleasing to God. The circle is endless.*

PRAYER: *Jesus Christ, God's Son, Savior (Ichthus), I find the idea of giving You satisfaction very empowering and motivating. Please show me, every day, another way to please You. Amen!*

> **I want to do those things that are pleasing to God, like loving my family, sharing with my friends, lifting my voice to God, thanking Him, doing what is right.**

INTERACT: How is predestination by God to Sonship (Ephesians 1:5) regulated by Paul's teaching in Romans 8:29–30?

_____
_____
_____
_____

How would you respond if someone claimed God is an egotistical glory hog?

_____
_____
_____
_____

Here is how I want my everyday life to result in worship for God:

_____
_____
_____
_____

DAY 56

BE A LITTLE JESUS

> "And we know that in all things God works for the good of those who love him, who have been called according to his purpose. ²⁹For those God foreknew he also predestined to be conformed to the image of his Son..."
> —Romans 8:28–29a

Your God–given purpose now, in this life, is to bring glory to God. How? Besides bringing pleasure to God, you can also glorify Him by Being Like Jesus.

During His time on Earth, Jesus was filled with divine purpose; committed to the Father's life principles; at peace with Himself and others; patient to a fault (though no fault was found in Him); a humble servant of God and His fellow man; the epitome of faithfulness; the picture of compassion; focused outside His own little circle on people around him. As a place to begin, that's not bad. And He will help you in the pursuit.

Another way to be like Jesus is to develop a character like His. The Apostle Paul listed love, joy, peace, patience, kindness, goodness, faithfulness, gentleness and self–control (Galatians 5:22–23a) as qualities the Holy Spirit wants to grow in you.

"God's ultimate goal for your life on Earth is not comfort, but character development" (Warren, *The Purpose Driven Life*, p. 173). God's first priority isn't your happiness; it's your holiness. He's not against your happiness, but He cares much more about who you are, in Jesus, than what you accumulate or how much fun you have. No one has ever been as holy as Jesus. You cannot work at being like Jesus and ignore holiness. There is nothing that glorifies God more than you Being Like Jesus.

WHAT'S THE POINT?: *The more you're like Jesus, the more you glorify God. Developing the character traits of Jesus is a high goal for any Jesus follower.*

PRAYER: *Dear Jesus, please show me the person You had in mind when You created me, then help me become that person. Amen!*

> By being like Jesus you are actually a "LITTLE Jesus" to others who may have difficulty seeing Him. How is it going?

INTERACT: How does "Imitation is the greatest form of flattery" fit into "being conformed to the image of" Jesus, God the Son?

_____
_____
_____
_____

Which character traits of Jesus are shining through in your life today?

_____
_____
_____
_____

Which three "fruit of the Spirit" core values (Galatians 5:22–23) do you want to develop to a higher level in the year ahead? How will you do it?

_____
_____
_____
_____

DAY 57
GO M.A.D.

"For we are God's masterpiece. He has created us anew in Christ Jesus, so that we can do the good things he planned for us long ago."
—Ephesians 2:10 NLT

Along with bringing pleasure to God and being like Jesus, you can glorify God by serving His total creation. Nothing is closer to God's heart than that. And remember that other people are a priceless part of God's creative project.

Edward Everett Hale wrote, "I am only one, but still I am one. I cannot do everything, but still I can do something; and because I cannot do everything, I will not refuse to do something that I can do."

We worry about the daily needs and desires we have. Often they consume most of our time and energy. Prayer time is often focused on physical problems, material needs and our own wants and wishes. These are not bad things to pray about, but how often do you pray for people who are without God in their lives? Or for Christians suffering for their faith? Or someone who has no one else to pray for them?

To live with an external focus is to serve God's total creation. And it warms God's heart when you turn outward in prayer and action.

God has promised to take care of physical problems, material needs and your inward desires, if you will put Him and His agenda first (Matthew 6:33). Put Him in first place, and He will take care of you lovingly.

Ron Hutchcraft was Youth for Christ director for all of New York City. He said on a radio broadcast that each day when his kids left for school, he would remind them, "Go 'M.A.D.' Make A Difference."

Tom Brokaw, dean of American news anchormen, said, "It's easy to make a buck. It's a lot tougher to make a difference."

WHAT'S THE POINT?: *You and I were created for the purpose of doing good deeds, which God prepared in advance for us to do.*

> Stop asking God to bless what you're doing. Find out what God's doing. It's already blessed.
> —Bono

PRAYER: *Dear God, please teach me to care about the things You care about most. Amen!*

INTERACT: I am being "created anew in Christ Jesus" (Ephesians 2:10) in these ways:

_____
_____
_____

_____

Here are several things that God cares about greatly. Does God care about what matters most to me?

_____
_____
_____

_____

With God's help, I will go M.A.D. in this way:

_____
_____
_____

_____

My prayer focus is revealed by this scale:

0	1	2	3	4	5	6	7	8	9	10

I only pray for myself	I only pray for others	Healthy prayers for self and others

DAY 58

THE SERVING PARADOX

> "I will praise God's name in song and glorify him with thanksgiving."
> —Psalm 69:30
>
> "Teach me your way, LORD, that I may rely on your faithfulness; give me an undivided heart, that I may fear your name. ¹² I will praise you, Lord my God, with all my heart; I will glorify your name forever. ¹³ For great is your love toward me…"
> —Psalm 86:11–13a

There are literally countless ways to serve God's total creation when you glorify Him. The people logging trees and the environmentalists planting trees are brothers and sisters, both serving God's creation. He expects them to live their lives as servants of God, not servants of self or a particular cause.

There are those who believe that Earth is a god. Created by God, of course, but worshiping His creation is simple idolatry. God inspired biblical writers to point out that seeing God's creation and doing good deeds are reasons to rejoice in Him and glorify the Creator, not His creation.

We are called to approach everything we do in life as though we are on a direct mission from God—because we are! The world's oldest occupation, gardening, is taking care of God's creation. It is a noble assignment.

You probably think of the Garden of Eden when you consider Adam's vocation. Since humankind is also part of God's creation, however, performing the myriad tasks that facilitate mankind's welfare is also included. Any duties that do not potentially harm others should fit into our worship of, and service to, God, mankind's welfare included.

Look at your life and ask, "Is this activity honoring and glorifying God? Or is it honoring and glorifying me?" To glorify God and accomplish our life's purpose, we cannot ignore this dichotomy.

WHAT'S THE POINT?: *Serving humankind fits perfectly into our purpose of glorifying God while here on Earth. Serving His total creation gives meaning and satisfaction to a creature designed to find and fulfill a reason to be here.*

> Lord, make me a meek, humble servant, eager to lift up the weak. My prayer should always be, 'Make me a servant today.'

PRAYER: *Dear God, please give me an unselfish heart that searches for creative ways to glorify You by serving Your total creation. Amen!*

INTERACT: My heart is "divided" (Psalm 86:11) in this way:

_____
_____
_____
_____

What does it mean to "fear God's name"?

_____
_____
_____
_____

Idolatry is anything that I place ahead of God. I need to watch out for this idolatry in my life:

_____
_____
_____
_____

DAY 59
LET THE PARTY BEGIN

> "For the Lord takes pleasure in His people; He will glorify the lowly with salvation. [5] The godly ones shall be jubilant in glory; They shall sing for joy... " [21]...'Well done, good and faithful servant! You have been faithful with a few things; I will put you in charge of many things. Come and share your master's happiness!'"
> —Psalm 149:4–5a; Matthew 25:21

During his first campaign for President, Donald Trump met with a group of Christian leaders. One asked him, "Have you ever confessed your sins?" He replied that he had not, because he never felt the need. Many are in that same boat. The idea that you need saving can feel awkward.

Enjoying God begins with surrendering to Jesus as your Savior. Before that, your relationship with God can only be incomplete, blurry and fragmented. "There is nothing more important than your eternal salvation," says actor Kirk Cameron. Being like Jesus builds on the foundation of being saved from your sin.

If someone wants to enjoy God but does not submit to the Savior, it's like those sprinters who literally jump the gun. The race is stopped and they line up again. The race can only continue if the start is right.

God's purpose is for your life, here on Earth. But it extends to eternity as well. Not only can mankind bring pleasure to God, but He enables you to enjoy Him forever. God is not selfish; He wants us to delight in Him, just as He enjoys us! Your enjoyment is not unimportant to Him. In fact, your attempts to give pleasure to God please Him mightily, even as they increase your joy. Still, God cares more about your holiness than your transient happiness.

The whole idea of enjoying God is foreign to most people. You may fear Him, be angry at Him, misunderstand Him, view Him as a complete mystery, take Him for granted, even reject or forget about Him. But enjoying God is beyond the wildest imaginings of many. God Himself hopes our relationship will become one of mutual pleasure and delight.

Some would say that all your experiences in human life are intended to prepare you for the day when your enjoyment of the Creator is complete, pure, unadulterated and endlessly joyful. So, let the party begin!

WHAT'S THE POINT?: *Your chief end (purpose) is to glorify God and enjoy Him forever. It all begins with salvation. In the eternal future your enjoyment of God will go on and on and...*

PRAYER: *Thank You, dear Lord, that we can enjoy You and our lives right now, besides all eternity. Show me opportunities to send that message to sullen, fearful, frustrated people all around me today. Amen!*

> "The Scotch catechism says that man's chief end is 'to glorify God and enjoy Him forever.' ...Fully to enjoy is to glorify. In commanding us to glorify Him, God is inviting us to enjoy Him."
> —C.S. Lewis, Reflections on the Psalms

INTERACT: In Matthew 25:21, what is God's reward for your faithfulness?

_____

_____

_____

_____

Have you or someone you know tried to obtain God's blessings without ever trusting Jesus as Savior? Did they jump the gun? What was the result?

_____

_____

People who never put their trust in Jesus are still blessed in this life in many ways. What are some of the ways God blesses unbelievers?

You might think salvation is all about eternity. But how can it bless your life right now?

- How would you explain the C.S. Lewis quotation in the box above?

DAY 60

RELATIONSHIPS ARE NOT WINE

> "A friend loves at all times... ⁹Perfume and incense bring joy to the heart, and the pleasantness of a friend springs from their heartfelt advice. ¹⁰Do not forsake your friend or a friend of your family, and do not go to your relative's house when disaster strikes you— better a neighbor nearby than a relative far away."
> —Proverbs 17:17a, 27:9–10

A professional couple decided to put off meaningful relationships in order to ensure the future. Both the husband, a lawyer, and his wife, a medical researcher, worked long hours and days to prepare for a great retirement. They hoped to amass enough money to retire early. Then they would enjoy the fruits of their long years of hard work.

They completely dedicated themselves to their jobs, aiming to call it quits by age fifty. They never took vacations; they hired a full-time nanny to raise the kids, servants to take care of the house and grounds; and dedicated themselves to seventy- and eighty-hour work weeks.

Finally, age fifty rolled around and they retired. But their children never came around, preferring to spend time with their old nanny and housekeeper. Then, to their chagrin, the couple discovered that they didn't even know each other anymore. They had deferred their most basic relationships until later, only to find that those relationships had dried up and blown away, like tumbleweeds with shallow roots licking the dust.

Unlike wine, storing your relationships in a dark, dusty room until later does not mellow them. They need light, warmth, and constant engagement in order to work right and provide benefits. It's true both in human relationships and with the divine God of the universe.

What are you waiting for? Enjoy your mutually satisfying connection with God today.

WHAT'S THE POINT?: *Relationships cannot be deferred; to be worthwhile in the future, they must be practiced and polished—and enjoyed—in the present!*

> "A real friend is one who walks in when the rest of the world walks out."
> —Walter Winchell

PRAYER: *Dear Lord Jesus, I want to enjoy my relationship with You right now. Please show me how. Amen!*

INTERACT: What pleasantness have you experienced from a friend who gave heartfelt advice (Proverbs 27:9)?

_____

_____

_____

One time I learned it is better to have a neighbor nearby than a relative far away (27:10) was:

_____

_____

_____

I have a stale relationship that is not getting better by being put on a shelf. I will do this to refresh it:

_____

_____

_____

Walter Winchell said a true friend 'walks in when others walk out.' Describe a time you experienced that truth:

___
___
___
___

DAY 61

GREEN-EYED GIRL

> But in your hearts revere Christ as Lord. Always be prepared to give an answer to everyone who asks you to give the reason for the hope that you have. But do this with gentleness and respect, ⁱ⁶keeping a clear conscience, so that those who speak maliciously against your good behavior in Christ may be ashamed of their slander.
> —1 Peter 3:15–16

Even tiny children understand jealousy. Maybe not *understand*, but at least they know what it feels like and how to *be* jealous.

Emily was two when her Daddy was deployed to Afghanistan. He would Zoom™ with his family every week, and Emily understood how precious her Dad was to her. When he surprised her at home for her third birthday, she was ecstatic. But she could not come to terms with sharing Daddy. When Mommy hugged and kissed Daddy, Emma pouted. When he held her five-year-old brother, she threw a tantrum. Emma was even green with envy when he played with the dog. She wanted to keep Daddy all for herself. And nobody else had better get in her way.

Many believers jealously guard their connection with Jesus, too. Enjoying Jesus unselfishly means you will cherish your friendship with Him so dearly that you will take 1 Peter 3:15 to heart. People around us whom we care about will reap great benefits from encountering Jesus. So, loving Him unselfishly is paramount to achieving your chief end—loving God and enjoying Him forever.

A salesman gave me a fistful of business cards, saying he would pay a finder's fee for every customer I steered his way. Jesus is overjoyed when you steer a friend or family member toward Him. There is a special blessing for those who share their faith with another. Think of it as caring about what God cares about most.

WHAT'S THE POINT?: *If you are in the process of becoming like Jesus, do not keep Him to yourself. There are many around you who are simply dying to know and enjoy Him.*

> **Witnessing for Jesus is simply one beggar telling another beggar where to find bread.**

PRAYER: *Precious Lord, You are so wonderful that I want my friends and family to know the exquisite pleasure of loving You too. Help me find the courage to explain my faith to them. Amen!*

INTERACT: I have gently explained to a questioner where my hope is placed. Here's the story:

_____
_____
_____

How effective is witnessing when a Christian treats an unbeliever disrespectfully?

_____
_____
_____

What are the three steps for sharing your faith, outlined in 1 Peter 3:15? *

* 1.) Have an answer ready; 2.) Clearly understand the hope you have in Jesus; and 3.) Treat the questioner gently and lovingly.

DAY 62

LOOK ON THE RIGHT SIDE

> I thank my God every time I remember you. ⁴In all my prayers for all of you, I always pray with joy ⁵because of your partnership in the gospel from the first day until now, ⁶being confident of this, that he who began a good work in you will carry it on to completion until the day of Christ Jesus.
> —Philippians 1:3–6

Maria was taking an evening walk with her father. Wonderingly, she looked up at the stars. "Oh, Daddy, if the wrong side of heaven is so beautiful, what will the right side be like?" (Charles L. Allen, *Home Fires*).

People ask, "Will my pet be in heaven? I cannot fathom living without her." Or they might say, "I love to golf. Do you think there will be golf courses in heaven?" I am tempted to rebut, "If your pet is not there, do you still want to go?" Or "Do you think heaven will be boring if you cannot play golf?"

The entire discussion is futile, because "…it is written: 'What no eye has seen, what no ear has heard, and what no human mind has conceived'—the things God has prepared for those who love him" (1 Corinthians 2:9). We are often confused about the comparative value of highly anticipated things. The eternal future for Jesus's followers is beyond comprehending. I cannot fully picture it. But it's going to be fantastic beyond imagining.

A tourist in Cairo was in an oriental rug shop in the souk. She marveled at the beautiful carpets, but was puzzled by an ugly, stringy mess hanging against the back wall. Noting the price tag, she was bewildered at how much it cost. So, she asked the shop owner why.

Silently, he turned the carpet over so she could see the front side. It was the most beautiful rug she had ever seen. "Ma'am," he explained, "you have been looking at the wrong side."

You and I can only see the underside of heaven; the right side is too profound for our earthbound minds to comprehend. It's just part of enjoying God forever.

WHAT'S THE POINT?: *God has made it easy to enjoy Him forever. Eternity will be filled with joys greater than any golf course or shopping mall. Trust Him.*

> "We do not need to speculate on what heaven will be like. It is enough to know that we will be forever with Him."
> —William Barclay

PRAYER: *God, thank You for making heaven so fabulous that we cannot imagine its glory. Amen!*

INTERACT: How would you characterize your partnership in the Gospel (the Good News)?

___

___

___

___

God has begun a good work in you; how is He carrying it through to completion?

___

___

___

___

Let me describe a time I looked at my circumstances from the wrong side. Here's how I discovered my mistake:

_____

_____

_____

_____

DAY 63

THAT FAR COUNTRY

> All these people were still living by faith when they died. They did not receive the things promised; they only saw them and welcomed them from a distance, admitting that they were foreigners and strangers on earth. ¹⁴People who say such things show that they are looking for a country of their own. ¹⁵If they had been thinking of the country they had left, they would have had opportunity to return. ¹⁶Instead, they were longing for a better country—a heavenly one. Therefore, God is not ashamed to be called their God, for he has prepared a city for them.
> —Hebrews 11:13–16

The closer people get to the end of life, the more they think about the next life. Most young people don't think very much about heaven. It seems so remote at that age.

When my wife, Kathy, was dying of interstitial lung disease (God healed her), we read a book by Billy Graham, called *Nearing Home*. He died, at age ninety-nine, even as we were reading it. Kathy and I felt closer to God after finishing it.

My sister, Anne, was eager to go home to heaven. Her earthly life had become unbearably painful and lonely. For an extended time, God did not grant our prayers for her. She soldiered on, longing to see Jesus face-to-face. At times you could think that God was unaware of her situation. Today she is with the Lord.

Leighton Ford told of a little boy who got on the elevator at the Empire State Building. He and his Daddy started to the top. They flashed past the floors: 10, 30, 50, 70. Soon he was nervous. "Daddy," he asked, "does God know we're coming?" (A sermon, *Hope for a Great Forever*).

Of course, God knows we're coming. We have been enjoying Him, and He us, here in the present. The future is a superlative heavenly version of this life that is preparation for an eternity of pure, undiluted joy, as you and God live out the eternal purpose for which you were created.

WHAT'S THE POINT?: *It took God only six days to create the universe. He has had about 2,000 years to work on heaven, the fabulous future home of His people. Won't Heaven be Grand?*

See 2 Peter 3:13, Isaiah 65:17, Revelation 21:1, *et al*. Also read John Burke's book, *Imagine Heaven*, for a glimpse of how wonderful we believe heaven will be.

PRAYER: *Lord God, please give me lots of opportunities to lay up treasures in heaven. And make it possible that I could take others with me. Amen!*

INTERACT: Hebrews 11 is called the Faith Chapter. What part of it is most inspiring to you?

_____
_____
_____
_____

Heaven can seem farther away than the Gobi Desert. I am doing this to make the reality of Heaven closer:

_____
_____
_____

I am making the most of God's purpose in my life. I bring joy to God and I have found my own joy by glorifying Him. Let me explain:

_____
_____
_____

DAY 64

TAKING STOCK

> If anyone, then, knows the good they ought to do and doesn't do it, it is sin for them.
> —James 4:17

Sin is wrongdoing, according to God's high standard. Humankind has made a science of sinning. But sin is also *not doing* the good thing you ought. Humans are adept at both sides of this sad equation.

As you become more like Jesus, ask yourself how you are doing, not only in avoiding wrongdoing, but also with your success at doing good things that God has planned in advance for you to do (Ephesians 2:10).

Today's essay offers the opportunity to examine your heart, especially in this area of glorifying God and enjoying Him now and throughout eternity. Ponder the following, which reflects on Chapter Five: "God's Glory and Pleasure."

If you want to rededicate yourself to God's purpose, to bring delight and pleasure to God, to enjoy God more, then tell Him so. And get ready to be surprised by the joy He breathes into your life.

WHAT'S THE POINT?: *A little self–examination should show you how well you are avoiding wrong-doing and pursuing good works in Jesus's name. He is honored by your introspective look.*

> "Your life is too valuable, your calling too great, and your God too awesome to waste your life on what doesn't matter."
> —Craig Groeschel

PRAYER: *Father in Heaven, show me what I can do to honor and glorify You more perfectly. That should bring both of us a lot of joy. Amen!*

INTERACT: I rate my progress toward being like Jesus as:

0	1	2	3	4	5	6	7	8	9	10
Zero progress				2 steps forward, 1 step back						Rapid progress

I think my life may be bringing pleasure to God in this way:

_____

_____

_____

_____

Ways that I serve God's creation:

_____

_____

_____

_____

To better fulfill my purpose of knowing God and enjoying Him forever, I will:

_____

_____

_____

_____

_____

6
HONEST TO GOODNESS

(Days 65–73)
To supplement your experience in Chapter Six, go to www.YouTube.com and listen to "Honesty" sung by Billy Joel (lyric video)

DAY 65

FAREWELL TO TRUST

> God is not a man, that he should lie, nor a son of man, that he should change his mind. Does he speak and then not act? Does he promise and not fulfill?
> —Numbers 23:19

Even in the hearts of secular people like Billy Joel, the desire for honesty can overwhelm. Untruth is thought to be a cancer in life, even by non-Christians. The desire for honesty and truth should be even stronger in the hearts of genuine Jesus followers.

The dictionary defines it like this: *honesty*, noun: uprightness; integrity; uncompromising adherence to moral and ethical principles; trustworthiness; truthfulness; sincerity.

Why is honesty so important? Because it's an essential part of God's nature. Dishonesty denies God's character in you. Anyone who hopes to become like Jesus must take seriously the nature and character of God. When you commit to Being Like Jesus, His essence becomes, more and more, yours. Paul reminded his readers to be imitators of God (Ephesians 5:1). Even a small fraud complicates the God–human relationship. It does not make Him stop being your Father, but it damages your fellowship with Him and with those around you. Dishonesty especially damages relationships with those you love the most.

Honesty is inseparably joined to trust. Trust is lost when deceit comes to light. Richard Nixon's presidency ended, not when it was learned that he had known about his minions breaking into the offices of the Democratic National Committee in the Watergate building. The American people lost trust in their President when they found out that he had tried to cover up his knowledge. It may take a thousand honest actions to earn trust, but only one dishonesty to poison a trust so carefully built.

Eleanor Roosevelt, one of the plainest–looking people in public service, said, "No matter how plain a woman may be, if truth and honesty are written across her face, she will be beautiful."

> "The most expensive thing in the world is trust. It can take years to earn and just a matter of seconds to lose."
> —Tupac Shakur

WHAT'S THE POINT?: *To be like Jesus, we must set and meet a high standard for honesty—in thought, word and action.*

PRAYER: *Dear God, it is so easy to fudge the truth, especially when I think someone will feel hurt, or when it seems dishonesty will benefit me. Lay Your honesty upon my heart. Amen!*

INTERACT: Human beings are prone to lying and to changing their minds (Numbers 23:19). How is your HQ (honesty quotient)?

_____
_____
_____
_____

Most people's dishonesty is a result of biblical compromise. I will resist such actions by doing this:

_____

_____

_____

Explain how someone's dishonesty damaged your trust in them:

_____

_____

_____

My standard for truthfulness is about here:

0	1	2	3	4	5	6	7	8	9	10
I'm never truthful					I'm often truthful					I'm always truthful

DAY 66

SLEEPING WITH THE DEVIL

> You belong to your father, the devil, and you want to carry out your father's desire. He was a murderer from the beginning, not holding to the truth, for there is no truth in him. When he lies, he speaks his native language, for he is a liar and the father of lies.
> —John 8:44

Not only does dishonesty poison our fellowship with God, but dishonesty also puts us in bed with the devil.

I know enough Greek that when our family drove around Athens and the Greek countryside, I constantly tried translating road signs from Greek to English. I couldn't stop! How tiring to read the signs and try communicating in another tongue. It was not my native language. It's exhausting to try operating in anything other than your mother tongue.

A Tanzanian friend has my respect and sympathy. Though he grew up in English schools, his native tongue is Swahili. He has to translate in his head before he speaks to us, because English is not his native language.

If we're God's children, truth should be our mother tongue. When we're untruthful, we're speaking Satan's lingua franca. He communicates in lies all the time—there's no such thing as truth in him. And we're sleeping with the enemy every time we tell an untruth.

To be like Jesus, you may have to adopt a whole new attitude toward truth and honesty. Sometimes you might "fudge" the truth, thinking it will spare people's feelings, or will gain you some advantage. Jesus said, "The truth will set you free" (John 8:32). Paul reminded his readers to speak the truth "in love" (Ephesians 4:15).

Speaking truth does not mean trampling on people's feelings. But we can never accomplish God's plan by being deceitful. It is one of the most common "Christian sins." Sometimes we think it best to avoid the truth; but that's not God's way, and it certainly is not Being Like Jesus.

WHAT'S THE POINT?: *To be like Jesus, take a strong position on honesty. Even when it might be awkward or uncomfortable, honesty is always the best policy.*

> "A lie gets halfway around the world before the truth has a chance to put its pants on."
> —Winston Churchill

PRAYER: *Holy Spirit, point out the tendency toward dishonesty in me. Help me build trust and integrity by valuing the truth. Amen!*

INTERACT: When I lie, I am speaking the devil's native language (John 8:44). That makes me feel:

_____
_____
_____
_____

The devil is "the father of lies" and has passed along the penchant for untruthfulness to us. How has that complicated your life?

_____
_____
_____
_____

Next time I am tempted to "fudge" the truth, I will do this to remember to be honest:

_____
_____
_____
_____

Explain the nuance in Winston Churchill's quotation above.

DAY 67

DEATH COMES TO LIFE

> Now the serpent was more crafty than any of the wild animals the Lord God had made. He said to the woman, "Did God really say, 'You must not eat from any tree in the garden'?" ²The woman said to the serpent, "We may eat fruit from the trees in the garden, ³but God did say, 'You must not eat fruit from the tree that is in the middle of the garden, and you must not touch it, or you will die. ⁴"You will not surely die," the serpent said to the woman.
> —Genesis 3:1–4

Dishonesty muddies life's most important truths. When our confidence in truth and untruth becomes murky, it muddies all of life.

How important was it for Adam and Eve to shape their actions according to God's truth? No other "little white lie" has caused such pain as the devil's little, "You will not surely die!"

Adam and Eve made a choice in response to this lie. Their simple action (how could eating a piece of fruit hurt?) is the source of every pain and woe known to humanity. Death itself came to life that day. Not until Jesus died on the cross and rose from the grave has eternal death relinquished its awful grip on humanity.

Satan's little lie muddied the simple fact that eating the fruit would result in death. The first couple ate, knowing it was rebellion against God, and death was unleashed.

"In the space between yes and no, there is a lifetime," writes Jodi Picoult. "It's the difference between the path you walk and one you leave behind; it's the gap between who you thought you could be and who you really are…"

The space between Adam's and Eve's *yes* and *no* has stretched to 6,000 years. The path they chose to walk truncated the perfection of their relationship with God. The disobedient couple thought they could be god. But who they really were is much less; just suckers duped by the evil one.

In his stellar book, *Decision Making and the Will of God*, Dr. Garry Friesen observes, "We want to make right decisions, for we realize that the decisions we make turn around and make us. As we choose one end of the road, we choose the other." *

WHAT'S THE POINT?: *Adam and Eve's decision to follow Lucifer instead of God underlies all the horrors of human history. Believing the lie has brought inexpressible tragedy to mankind. Jesus's death and resurrection provide the only way to rise above.*

> "Your choices are made in a moment, and yet their consequences transcend a lifetime."
> —MJ DeMarco

PRAYER: *God, give me courage to stand against the dishonesty of the evil one. Please reveal Your truth, and with it, set me free. Amen!*

INTERACT: In Genesis 3:1–4, the devil used a two-step approach to tempt Eve. What are the steps?

___

___

___

___

Situational ethics denies moral and ethical absolutes. Here is one such situation I know about:

___

___

___

___

Describe Jodi Picoult's "gap between who you thought you were, and who you really are":

_____

_____

_____

_____

* Friesen, Garry, *Decision Making and the Will of God*, p. 6

DAY 68

SEPARATION ANXIETY

> Then the man and his wife heard the sound of the Lord God as he was walking in the garden in the cool of the day, and they hid from the Lord God among the trees of the garden. ⁹But the Lord God called to the man, "Where are you?" ¹⁰He answered, "I heard you in the garden, and I was afraid because I was naked; so I hid." And he said, "Who told you that you were naked?...
> —Genesis 3:8–11a

Besides the damage that dishonesty does by muddying life's most important truths, it also separates us from God and others. Genesis 3 has been questioned, even ridiculed by doubters, because it utters a damning condemnation against sin. The ugly account reveals the effects of human disobedience against God. Dishonesty clearly qualifies as sin, and will result in many painful separations from Him and from others.

Jesus explained that to love God is to obey Him (John 14:15, 21). He said, "If you love me, you will obey what I command...Whoever has my commands and obeys them, he is the one who loves me." That can only mean that disobeying God proves we do not love Him as we should. Dishonesty is a damning disobedience against God.

Some believe they are intentionally separated from God and doing just fine, never realizing that God is still intimately involved in their existence. From air to breathe to good jobs, from creation to the love of family and friends, God blesses even unbelievers.

But dishonesty often causes irreconcilable differences in families, churches, workplaces and nations. Ultimate separation from God comes when you reach the end of life without reconciling with Him. Do not let that happen. Work tirelessly to bring reconciliation between your loved ones and God. Trust the freeing power of truth.

WHAT'S THE POINT?: *Dishonesty is one major component in mankind's separation from God. But God is eager to reconcile. And He gives a ministry of reconciliation to Jesus's followers* (2 Corinthians 5:19–20).

> "When Jesus paid for our sins on the cross, the veil in the temple that symbolized our separation from God, was split from top to bottom, indicating that direct access to God was once again available."
> —Rick Warren

PRAYER: *God of all things, please remove my separation from you and from others. Nurture my spirit of ethical integrity. Amen!*

INTERACT: When God asked, "How did you know you were naked?" Adam's sin was disrobed. How did their relationship change at that moment?

_____

_____

_____

Describe a situation where trouble could have been avoided by the simple use of honesty:

_____

_____

_____

_____

Refute the claim, "Lying was better because the truth would have hurt their feelings":

_____
_____
_____
_____

Truthfulness reveals maturity, according to Ephesians 4:15. Elaborate:

_____
_____
_____
_____

DAY 69
THE BOOK OF WISDOM

> But now you must also rid yourselves of all such things as these: anger, rage, malice, slander, and filthy language from your lips. [9]Do not lie to each other, since you have taken off your old self with its practices [10]and have put on the new self, which is being renewed in knowledge in the image of its Creator.
> —Colossians 3:8–10

A *USA Today* poll found that only fifty–six percent of Americans teach honesty to their children. And a Louis Harris poll revealed the distressing fact that sixty–five percent of high school students polled said they would cheat on an important exam if they could get away with it.

A noted physician appeared on a network talk show and proclaimed, "Lying is an important part of social life, and children who are unable to do it are children who may have developmental problems" (*Daily Bread*, September 23, 1991). Who could be surprised? The fallen, sinful human nature will lie and cheat, unless either taught not to, or reformed by the power of God.

The question persists, "How can I become more honest?" There are several things that contribute to personal integrity. One is to set a high personal standard for honesty up–front. Decide, going in, that nothing less than scrupulous honesty is acceptable. Soon enough you will be known for your honesty, and that will help you stay the course.

Don't wait until the pressure is on to decide how honest you will be. It's probably too late by then. Your exam will be in the Proctor's hands and if you cheat, you will ultimately fail His test. Decide right now that God's yardstick will be yours. Accept no less than God's standard of complete honesty—it's a decisive element in Being Like Jesus.

WHAT'S THE POINT?: *Being a person of integrity opens your life to all kinds of blessings from God, that the liar or cheater will never get.*

> "Honesty is the first chapter in the book of wisdom."
> —Thomas Jefferson
> *Letter to Nathaniel Macon, 1819*

PRAYER: *Blessed Lord, please make me an honest-to-goodness truth-teller. And give me opportunities to teach and model honesty for others. Amen!*

INTERACT: "Lying to each other" was a product of the "old self" (Colossians 3:9). How do you still need to work on that, with God's help?

_____

_____

_____

_____

When you "put on the new self, which is being renewed in knowledge in the image of the Creator" (Colossians 3:10), what changed immediately?

_____

_____

_____

_____

What changed over time?

_____

_____

_____

_____

I have received these blessings and bonuses from God because I practiced truthfulness:

_____

_____

_____

_____

DAY 70

WHAT IS YOUR HONESTY QUOTIENT?

> A good man brings good things out of the good stored up in him, and an evil man brings evil things out of the evil stored up in him. **36 But I tell you that everyone will have to give account on the day of judgment for every empty word they have spoken. 37 For by your words you will be acquitted, and by your words you will be condemned."**
> —Matthew 12:35–37

You may be wondering, "How can I be more honest?" Good question. First, decide up-front to utilize God's high standard. Next, make a habit of analyzing your thoughts and words and actions, looking for any hint of impropriety.

The place to start being scrupulously honest is in your thoughts, even before words are verbalized or actions are engaged. The mind is the starting point for every decision, including those related to honesty. Lucifer played skillfully with Eve's mind and finally instigated an act of rebellion.

The human heart is the culprit. Old Testament prophet Jeremiah pointed out, under inspiration from the Holy Spirit, that the heart is deceitful above all else. "Who," he asks, "can understand it?" (Jeremiah 17:9)

Dishonesty includes the words you speak. Even small "fibs" can be damaging. A "little white lie" is neither little nor harmless. When I was stationed in Hawaii, the prostitutes of Honolulu lined up along Ala Moana Boulevard, protesting because their specialty was a "victimless crime," they claimed. Many feel similarly about the little white lie. Yet God says it is evil and must be expunged. Oral dishonesty can include saying nothing, ironically, when you should speak up.

Deceit can be conveyed through actions without words ever being spoken. A careful analysis of your words and actions will reveal your honesty quotient. This analysis takes very little time. Each night as your head hits the pillow, ask God to identify anything that did not measure up to His standard that day. You may be sure that He will tell you.

WHAT'S THE POINT?: *Seek God's purification of your thoughts, words and actions related to honesty. It is a transformation He is eager to apply to your heart.*

> "But if thought corrupts language, language can also corrupt thought."
> —George Orwell, *1984*

PRAYER: *Father in heaven, show me how to control my thoughts, which lead to words and actions that either honor or dishonor You. Amen!*

INTERACT: If you will be required to account for every empty word (Matthew 12:36), how will that influence what you say?

_____
_____
_____

If thoughts are the seeds of my words and actions, I need to keep my mind clean and wholesome by:

_____
_____
_____
_____

One time I was deceitful by not speaking up was:

_____
_____
_____
_____

I rate my honesty quotient about here:

0	1	2	3	4	5	6	7	8	9	10
I lie com–pulsively				White lies sneak in sometimes					I am scrupu–lously honest	

DAY 71
WOUNDED BY FRIENDS

> Better is open rebuke than hidden love. ⁶ Wounds from a friend can be trusted, but an enemy multiplies kisses.
> Proverbs 27:5–6

One very important component in the matrix of honesty is to install lie detectors in your life. Recruit people you trust to hold you accountable. They must know Scripture, have a vibrant relationship with God, and be trustworthy with your secrets.

Give others permission to ask, "Is that the total, complete truth, so help you God?" If you really want this to work, give your spouse, siblings, and/or kids permission to ask you that. What a wonderful teaching tool in young, impressionable lives. Your complete honesty can be a legacy for your wider circle of influence for generations to come.

Go on record with friends, family and co-workers that you are raising the standard for your own honesty. As you institute greater honesty in your daily thoughts, words and actions, it will become easier and easier to be truthful.

If you know your lie detector loves you, they can say anything you need to hear, even when it's painful to receive. If you're wounded by a true friend, the injury will heal. If you reject a friend's gentle correction, the friendship may falter, and you will still have to deal with the initial problem, dishonesty.

By giving permission for others to be your lie detector, you will take a giant step toward godly honesty.

WHAT'S THE POINT?: *Lie detectors help get at the truth. Yours could assist you to become ever more like Jesus.*

PRAYER: *Dear Jesus, please point me toward someone who will help me overcome dishonesty. I sincerely mean it. Amen!*

INTERACT: Describe a time when a foe treated you falsely:

> "It's discouraging to think how many people are shocked by honesty and how few by deceit."
> —Noël Coward, *Blithe Spirit*

_____
_____
_____

On the flip side, when did a friend offer constructive criticism that hurt but helped in the end?

_____
_____
_____

I want to give the personal honesty "lie detector" a try. A person I trust who could help me (name please) is:

_____
_____
_____

Write your own personal prayer to express your trust in God to become more honest.

_____
_____
_____
_____

DAY 72
BIBLE FEAST

> My prayer is not that you take them out of the world but that you protect them from the evil one. [16]They are not of the world, even as I am not of it. [17]Sanctify them by the truth; your word is truth.
> —John 17:15–17

The word of God is the greatest treasury of truth the world has ever known. To tap into God's storehouse of truthful honesty, feast on daily helpings of Scripture. Ask God to reveal His sure truth to you as you pick up your Bible. Every word is truth, though not every truth in the universe is reported in the Bible (i.e., πr^2 or $E=MC^2$). There are many approaches to imbibing truth from God's Word. There are also many resources that will help you.

Read the Bible through in a year (or two if you need more time). Three-and-one-quarter chapters a day will cover all 1,189 chapters in 365 days. *Our Daily Bread,* the American Bible Society, and other resources have tools to help you stay on-track.

Carry out in-depth study of smaller portions, using the many study helps available, like concordances, dictionaries, translation aids and commentaries. There are many printed or online studies about particular subjects or portions of Scripture that offer valuable guidance.

Online Bible services such as YouVersion™ and Bible Gateway™ publish *Bible reading plans* on many subjects that you can follow right on your phone.

Immerse yourself in Scripture by *memorizing important Bible passages* that will stay with you forever; all in the interest of enjoying a Bible banquet fit for a gourmet. If you are installing a personal lic detector in your life, ask her or him to help you prepare this delicious, life-transforming scriptural repast. God is eager to guide you.

WHAT'S THE POINT?: *Of all the steps you can take to enhance your honesty, the Bible is first. Use it to become more like Jesus.*

> "Whether we are reading the Bible for the first time or standing in a field in Israel next to a historian and an archaeologist and a scholar, the Bible meets us where we are. That is what truth does."
> —Rob Bell, *Velvet Elvis*

PRAYER: *Blessed Redeemer, please lay out a feast of Bible truth for me to enjoy and share with other hungry people. It will enhance my honesty more than any other single thing. Amen!*

INTERACT: Can Jesus say of you, "they are not of the world, even as I am not of it" (John 17:16)? If not, what is your next course of action?

_____

_____

_____

Here's how God's Word sets me apart for a sacred use (*sanctify*, John 17:17)?

_____

_____

_____

Some claim the Bible is full of contradictions. Research this idea and jot some notes to answer this objection. (Hint: ask them to cite a specific example.):

_____

_____

I am going to memorize this Bible passage in the days and weeks ahead:

DAY 73

A COOKED GOOSE

> So, if you think you are standing firm, be careful that you don't fall! ¹³No temptation [or *testing or trial*] has overtaken you except what is common to mankind. And God is faithful; he will not let you be tempted beyond what you can bear. But when you are tempted, he will also provide a way out so that you can endure it.
> —1 Corinthians 10:12–13

As our culture becomes less Christian and more secular, will we buy into the popular belief that honesty in thoughts, words, and actions is optional? Will we become part of the slippery slide into untruth and damaged credibility? Will the whole realm of veracity be lost in Jesus Christ's body, the Church?

In *The Rated 'R' Church*, Shea Oakley writes, "The result of this drift towards casual worldliness may be the slow death of the mainstream evangelical church in America."

George Barna uses the so-called frog in the kettle idea to illustrate what may eventually happen. If a frog touches boiling water, it will immediately feel the scalding heat and attempt to hop out. But, put the same frog in room temperature water and very slowly heat it; the frog will not respond. In fact, it will enjoy the warm bath in the kettle until the gradually-heating water cooks its goose.

As the church gradually becomes accustomed to the ungodly popular culture, true Christianity, with its radical call to holiness, will be displaced by a religion that is Christian in name only.

This drift toward the devil's way of thinking is painfully apparent in the realm of honesty. To be like Jesus, you have to set and keep high standards of honesty in your thoughts, words and actions. Anything short of that is blatant, outright disobedience against God.

WHAT'S THE POINT?: *Lying might seem convenient, even preferable to the truth, in some situations. But God never approves, and He is calling the shots.*

> "In a time of deceit, telling the truth is a revolutionary act."
> — (Attributed to) George Orwell

PRAYER: *Lord of all, I am determined to be Your ambassador. Honesty is an integral part of that. Thank You for Your help. Amen!*

INTERACT: Use the following scale to rate your own honesty:

0	1	2	3	4	5	6	7	8	9	10
Prefer to lie					Part–time honesty					Always honest

Here is how I will analyze my honesty regularly:

_____
_____
_____

I have experienced a church that is slowly sinking into cultural relativism. Here is the story:

_____
_____
_____

This is my "menu" for feasting on daily Bible truth:

_____
_____
_____

7
FOLLOW THROUGH

(Days 74–87)
To enhance your experience in Chapter Seven, go to www.YouTube.com and listen to "This I Believe" sung by the Creed (lyric video)

DAY 74
DEATH AND TAXES

> "[Christ] has appeared once for all at the culmination of the ages to do away with sin by the sacrifice of himself. ^{27}Just as people are destined to die once, and after that to face judgment, ^{28}so Christ was sacrificed once to take away the sins of many; and he will appear a second time, not to bear sin, but to bring salvation to those who are waiting for him." —Hebrews 9:26–28

During the COVID-19 pandemic, with the government controlling citizens' everyday lives, the old saying, "Nothing is sure but death and taxes" took on new gravity. And while one political party has been labeled "tax and spend" by the other, both parties have shown themselves adept at that practice. From before Jesus's birth, taxes were a reality. After all, taxes are why Joseph and Mary were in Bethlehem that amazing night. Death is even more inevitable.

Answering the question, "What happens after I die?" is imperative. All of us will die someday. Some will live to a ripe old age, others will die suddenly, unexpectedly. As I wrote today's essay, 99-year-old Betty White just died. Nothing is sure except death and...

As we ponder what happens after we die, it helps to "Think Like Jesus." What happens to you *after* you die depends completely on what you do *before* you die. A golf pro can watch your follow-through (what your body and club do *after* you swing) and know what you did wrong *before* you hit the ball.

It's difficult to be objective about yourself. We often need someone else to help us know where we went wrong. Do you have a godly mentor? As you work at being like Jesus, you might need some help when it comes to the question, "What happens in the next life?" Finding someone to guide your trek just makes sense.

> "You can't go back and change the beginning, but you can start where you are and change the ending."
> —C. S. Lewis

WHAT'S THE POINT?: *What happens after I die depends entirely on my decisions, choices and actions before I die. Did I trust Jesus Christ as my Savior and live in a relationship with Him?*

PRAYER: *Lord God, please point me toward someone who is willing and able to guide me toward being more like Jesus. Amen!*

INTERACT: Being as objective as possible, I believe that after my death, God's judgment of me will be:

_____
_____
_____
_____

I agree that certain decisions greatly impact "what happens after I die." My follow through shows this about that:

_____
_____
_____
_____

What faithful Christian who cares about me might be able to help me prepare for the next life?

_____
_____
_____
_____

BTW, *Imagine Heaven* by John Burke (Baker Books, 2015) paints a wonderful picture of heaven.

_____
_____
_____
_____

DAY 75

GETTING PHYSICAL

> "Why were you searching for me?" he asked. "Didn't you know I had to be in my Father's house?" ⁵⁰But they did not understand what he was saying to them. ⁵¹Then he went down to Nazareth with them and was obedient to them. But his mother treasured all these things in her heart. ⁵²And Jesus grew in wisdom and stature, and in favor with God and man.
> —Luke 2:49–52

There are four 'realms' in each human life, including Jesus's (Luke 2:52). They are mental–emotional (wisdom), physical (stature), spiritual (in favor with God), and social (in favor with man). In terms of human nature, let's examine two of these realms within one person.

We will start with the physical nature, since it is most familiar to us. You know about this one. It's where you function, day in and day out. It's where you experience the world around you, where you find your greatest challenges and the most familiarity. Aching joints and shortness of breath point to it.

Ask people what they like least about themselves. At or near the top will be issues of physical appearance. "I hate my big nose." "I wish I could change my body's shape." "I look at an M&M and gain five pounds."

You seldom hear someone say, "I'm too selfish." Or "I think only about myself." Or, "I'm way too kind. I should be meaner." Or how about, "I wish I were less generous. I should keep more stuff for my own conspicuous consumption."

Many feel trapped in the material world. Something inside tells them there are more important things than the physical realm. But moving beyond time and space, health and pleasure to things of the heart and the welfare of others seems too difficult even to contemplate.

Jesus, our example and standard, lived successfully in all realms of human experience and being like Jesus means balancing your spiritual nature with the many aspects of life here and now. Gaining balance between all aspects of human life is tricky, but crucial.

WHAT'S THE POINT?: *We cannot escape physical demands without leaving this world. But we will be more successful and satisfied in life only if we can balance physical life with the mental–emotional, spiritual and social aspects of existence.*

PRAYER: *Lord and Savior Jesus Christ, I need Your help to balance my life, giving the right emphasis to each realm of human existence. Amen!*

> **"The 7 Social Sins: Wealth without work. Pleasure without conscience. Knowledge without character. Commerce without morality. Science without humanity. Worship without sacrifice. Politics without principle."**
> —From a sermon by Frederick Lewis Donaldson at Westminster Abbey, London, March 20, 1925

INTERACT: What did Jesus mean by "My Father's business" (Luke 2:49)?

_____

_____

_____

_____

One source of great internal conflict is ignoring the spiritual aspect of life. How could you help someone awaken to spiritual things?

_____

_____

_____

_____

My current reality puts these four aspects (Luke 2:52) in this order:

_____

_____

_____

_____

DAY 76

PICKUP TRUCKS ARE 'SPIRITUAL'

> Finally, be strong in the Lord and in his mighty power. [11] Put on the full armor of God, so that you can take your stand against the devil's schemes. [12] For our struggle is not against flesh and blood, but against the rulers, against the authorities, against the powers of this dark world and against the spiritual forces of evil in the heavenly realms. [13] Therefore put on the full armor of God, so that when the day of evil comes, you may be able to stand your ground, and after you have done everything, to stand.
> —Ephesians 6:10–13

I had the distinct privilege of visiting Tibet, the "Rooftop of the World." The most remarkable thing I learned was the Tibetans' attitude toward the spiritual, as contrasted with the physical aspect of reality. They truly seem to believe that the spiritual realm ranks above the physical.

The spiritual nature is less obvious than the physical, but no less real. Most Eastern religions elevate spiritual over physical. To Westerners, matters of a spiritual nature may be ignored, discounted, or even ridiculed. Anyone who says they will not believe something unless they experience it with the human senses is a dictionary specimen of a materialist.

Another facet of Western spirituality is that it can mean almost anything. A TV commercial showed a man on a mountaintop, leaning against his pickup, saying, "To me, trucks are spiritual." Until they break down or crash, or run out of fuel, of course.

The human spiritual nature is both sensitive and conscious. The Bible describes the soul as thirsty for God (Psalm 63:1), benefiting from wisdom (Proverbs 24:14), and a source of intense emotional response—another realm of human experience (Matthew 26:38).

Our daily choices affect our spiritual well-being. Emphasizing the physical realm of human life over the spiritual brings frustration, unhappiness, even dysfunction to life. The happiest people are those in whom spiritual godliness transcends life's physical, social or mental-emotional aspects.

If you want to become like Jesus, you cannot devalue the human spiritual nature without significantly damaging yourself mentally, spiritually and socially, both now and in the future.

> "...poverty in the West is a different kind of poverty. It is not only a poverty of loneliness but also of spirituality. There's a hunger for love, as there is a hunger for God."
> —Mother Teresa

WHAT'S THE POINT?: *To God, the highest order of existence is the spiritual. Physical life is brief. Mental-emotional life may be unstable, social life can be notional. Spiritual life, however, goes on eternally, in one place or another.*

PRAYER: *Holy Spirit, please make me aware of, and attuned to spiritual things. It is there that I connect on the deepest level with You. Amen!*

INTERACT: How are you struggling against the rulers and powers of the spiritual forces of evil (Ephesians 6:11)?

___

I experienced a "spiritual reality" that grabbed my attention. It was:

Describe how you have seen what Mother Teresa called a poverty of spirituality:

_____
_____
_____
_____

DAY 77

THAT NEST IN YOUR HAIR

> ...if you think you are standing firm, be careful that you don't fall! ¹³No temptation has overtaken you except what is common to mankind. And God is faithful; he will not let you be tempted beyond what you can bear. But when you are tempted, he will also provide a way out so that you can endure it.
> —1 Corinthians 10:12b–13

There is a deep-seated problem within the human heart. It is a problem with our two natures, physical and spiritual. The war between our two natures started with Satan's rebellion.

The Bible teaches that Lucifer, one of the archangels, rebelled against God. Lucifer tried to overthrow God and become the supreme spiritual being in the universe (see Isaiah 14:12–15). He managed to convince one-third of the angels to join his insidious revolt. In the ensuing conflict Lucifer (the devil, Satan) and his angels were defeated and cast out of heaven (Revelation 12).

Since that time, he has made war on God's creation, including you and me. Adam's and Eve's disobedience was the beginning of all our problems with sin.

True to his original aim, Satan is devoted to two things, undermining God as Supreme Ruler of the universe; and destroying God's creation, especially humankind (1 Peter 5:8).

The devil cannot force us to sin, but he can make life miserable. And he can dig many potholes in our path. Martin Luther nailed it when he observed, "You cannot keep birds from flying over your head, but you do not have to let them build a nest in your hair."

WHAT'S THE POINT?: *From that fateful day in Eden, it has been sin versus holiness, evil opposing good. Being Like Jesus guarantees an ongoing conflict. Only Jesus's sacrifice on the cross and His resurrection give us hope.*

> Mark Twain spoke for many when he said, "I can resist anything but temptation."

PRAYER: *Jesus, please pray for me as I face the devil's forces of evil. I want victory in my pursuit of Being Like Jesus. Amen!*

INTERACT: Have you ever felt strong in your faith, only to crash and burn (1 Corinthians 10:12b)? How did you recover?

_____
_____
_____
_____

If you have thought that by giving in to temptation, life will be smoother, then you have heard the voice of Satan. What did he tell you?

_____
_____
_____
_____

Better yet, what did you tell him?

_____
_____
_____
_____

It seems that my whole life is one conflict after another, between good and evil. My only hope for victory is:

_____
_____
_____
_____

The same Greek word (πειρασμός—*peirasmos*) is translated *temptation*, *testing*, and *trial*. What does this tell you about the Bible and life?

_____
_____
_____
_____

DAY 78

UGLY AS SIN

> Therefore, there is now no condemnation for those who are in Christ Jesus, ²because through Christ Jesus the law of the Spirit who gives life has set you free from the law of sin and death. ³For what the law was powerless to do because it was weakened by the flesh, God did by sending his own Son in the likeness of sinful flesh to be a sin offering. And so he condemned sin in the flesh.
> —Romans 8:1–3

It used to be, most knew what sin was. Even unbelievers could identify right from wrong. If you could not articulate a definition of sin, you still knew it when you saw it (or *did* it).

There is little idea of what sin really is in today's post–Christian society; even whether such a thing as sin exists. The Bible uses the word "sin" more than a thousand times, sixty-three times in Romans alone. A few of those references declare that sin is anything less than the perfection of God (Romans 3:23); it is rebellion against God (13:2); sin is rejection of the truth (2:8); the wages of sin are death (6:23); death is the product of sin (5:12) and so on.

People may disagree about what sin is, but we can all agree, sin is really easy to do (it takes no practice). Righteousness, on the other hand, takes constant training, self-discipline, practice, and work. It is easier just to give in, but you won't like the life that "giving in" produces.

Sin is the polar opposite of righteousness, which is simply defined as "right living according to God's Word."

A majority of Americans believe that just being good will outweigh their bad behavior. I taught comparative religions in colleges for many years and can confidently state that only Christianity has anything resembling grace, all God's blessings we do not deserve and cannot earn. Philip Yancey, in his wonderful book, *What's So Amazing About Grace*, explains that grace covers the fact you cannot do anything that makes God love you more—or less.

The Bible says that all our righteous acts are, literally, like filthy rags (Isaiah 64:6). In other words, it's impossible to act good enough to please a perfect God. Only Jesus's death and resurrection can make us right with God.

> "...a Christian is not a man who never goes wrong, but a man who is enabled to repent and pick himself up and begin over again after each stumble—because the Christ-life is inside him..."
> —C.S. Lewis, *Mere Christianity*

WHAT'S THE POINT?: *As ugly as sin is, God saves us by His grace. The death sentence is commuted, the death-row inmate is pardoned, and God redeems the lost for eternity.*

PRAYER: *Thank You, Lord God, for dealing with the horror of sin, thereby making a way that I can enjoy the pleasure of a relationship with You. Amen!*

INTERACT: Even believers struggle with sin. Thank God that "The law of the Spirit who gives life has set you free from the law of sin and death." Explain a recent victory in Jesus:

_____
_____
_____
_____

Describe the training, self-discipline, practice, and work you do regularly to win your struggles against sin:

_____
_____
_____
_____

Explain the implications of the definition, "righteousness is right living, according to God's word" (don't miss the two elements):

_____
_____
_____
_____

I am ☐ troubled ☐ comforted by the idea that there is nothing I can do to make God love me more or less. Here's what I mean:

_____
_____
_____
_____

DAY 79

CAN YOU AFFORD IT?

> **When you were slaves to sin, you were free from the control of righteousness. ²¹ What benefit did you reap at that time from the things you are now ashamed of? Those things result in death! ²² But now that you have been set free from sin and have become slaves of God, the benefit you reap leads to holiness, and the result is eternal life. ²³ For the wages of sin is death, but the gift of God is eternal life in Christ Jesus our Lord.**
> **—Romans 6:20–23**

Most of us will admit that sin has its pleasures. The Hebrews author wrote that Moses chose to suffer with his fellow Hebrews rather than enjoy the fleeting pleasures of sinful living (Hebrews 11:25).

Sin is too costly to afford if you look at the long-term price, compared to the short-term pleasure. Maybe you have paid a high price for the car (or house) of your dreams, then discovered that it didn't make you as happy as you expected. Most of us have done something similar. With the dream house or car, it's hard to predict how much pleasure you might get, over time. But there is no mystery about the brevity of sin's pleasures.

Years ago, when AIDS was still a new thing, a twenty-year-old woman was quoted in the *Detroit Free Press*. She was distraught that her life would soon end. She said, "I just wanted some fun, to enjoy a little sex. Now I have to die for it?"

Since Adam and Eve, the human tendency has been to trivialize sin—to minimize its danger and harm, or to shift the blame. It's one of the devil's most common lies. "Sin, if there even is such a thing, is unimportant," he whispers. "Don't give it another thought. Make a joke about it and move on."

We label sin as little white lies, weakness, a lapse of judgment, a mistake, a brief fling, sowing our wild oats. Or, in a famous comedian's twisted rationalizing, it's a "rendezvous."

God says the soul that sins will die (Ezekiel 18:4). Sin causes suffering to the sinner and brings pain and sorrow to everyone around them.

Hate evil and stick like super glue to what is good (Romans 12:9). The cost of sin, in self–inflicted damage and the fair and equal judgment of God, is exorbitant. No one can afford it.

WHAT'S THE POINT?: *Sin promises much but delivers little. Refuse to believe the devil's lie that sin is no big deal. Eternal punishment is too high a price to pay for a brief fling with evaporating pleasure.*

> **Pity the person who knows the price of everything but the value of nothing.**

PRAYER: *God in heaven, please help me take the long view, to avoid the eternal pain of punishment for defying You. Amen!*

INTERACT: One thing I used to do that now makes me feel ashamed is:

_____
_____
_____
_____

Compare the similarity of a fishhook to the lures of sin. Write (or verbalize) a paragraph making the point:

_____
_____
_____
_____

Rationalizing your wrongdoing never removes the guilt and pain. Explain your vacillations about sinning.

_____
_____
_____
_____

DAY 80

THE MEGAWATT POWER OF FORGIVENESS

> [19]But Joseph said to [his brothers], "Don't be afraid. Am I in the place of God? [20]You intended to harm me, but God intended it for good to accomplish what is now being done, the saving of many lives. [21]So then, don't be afraid. I will provide for you and your children." And he reassured them and spoke kindly to them.
> —Genesis 50:19–21

This wonderful Bible story reveals the power of *forgiveness*. Webster defines this good old church word as: to grant pardon for an offense or sin; to cancel a debt; to…pardon a person; to stop feeling resentment against someone.

Joseph, a distant ancestor of Jesus, had been sold by his jealous brothers into slavery. First, he was purchased by a government official and rose to prominence in that man's household. When he refused the sexual advances of the man's wife, he was unjustly imprisoned on her lie. Then, he proved to be such a great manager that his jailers put him in charge. Finally, he predicted a terrible famine and how to survive it. Finding no one else so qualified, Pharaoh promoted Joseph to Prime Minister of Egypt.

Now, their father was dead, and the brothers figured Joseph would finally get his revenge. They fell before him and offered themselves as slaves. But in a godly act, he forgave his scheming siblings. After many years of hardship, struggle and frustration, he could see God's greater plan. Forgiveness was a necessary element of what was next for Joseph.

God always has something good up His sleeve. If you trust Him, and if you follow through, He will reward you with unexpected, unpredictable blessings.

Didn't I tell you? *Forgiveness* is a wonderful old church word.

WHAT'S THE POINT?: *Forgiveness has such power that you can expect God to bless you in some surprising ways. Together, patience and forgiveness will lift you to a higher elevation.*

> "You meant to hurt me, but God had other ideas. Look how many lives have been saved!"
> —Joseph ben Israel

PRAYER: *Lord of heaven and Earth, please enrich my forgiving with the attitude of forgiveness You have toward me. I will wait patiently for You. Amen!*

INTERACT: When human logic says God is unkind or unfair, how do Joseph's words, "You intended to harm me, but God intended it for good" (Genesis 50:20) reaffirm your trust in God's faithful goodness?

_____
_____
_____
_____

What are some parallels between Joseph's story and Jesus's story?

_____
_____
_____
_____

Describe the greatest struggle with forgiveness you have ever faced.

_____
_____
_____
_____

Here is a time that God seemed unkind and/or unfair to me. Now I know I can trust Him:

_____

_____

_____

_____

DAY 81

LIVE GRACE FULL

> "...for all have sinned and fall short of the glory of God, ²⁴and all are justified freely by his grace through the redemption that came by Christ Jesus."
> —Romans 3:23–24
>
> "Each of you should use whatever gift you have received to serve others, as faithful stewards of God's grace in its various forms."
> —1 Peter 4:10

The most influential book in my life, after the Bible, is Philip Yancey's *What's So Amazing About Grace?* I was raised in a Christian tradition that seemed to focus mostly on God's judgment. So, grace has been a delightful, liberating discovery.

Lee Strobel wrote that *Justice* is getting what you deserve. *Mercy* is *not* getting what you deserve. *Grace* is getting what you *do not* deserve. Grace is "all God's blessings you do not deserve and cannot earn."

God not only extends grace to you, He expects you to extend grace to other people who do not deserve it. We don't merit God's forgiveness, and we cannot earn it—He offers it free of charge.

He offers *forgiveness* to your worst enemy as well. In many minds, that's the dark side of grace. Adolf Hitler would be in heaven if he repented of his many horrifying sins, and trusted Jesus as Savior before he died. That would qualify as God's grace, indeed. What do you think about that? Tough to swallow, huh? Unless your beloved child did some horrible thing. Or your best friend. Or you. Then, grace does not seem quite so dark.

Chuck Swindoll writes, "Grace has to be the loveliest word in the English language. It embodies almost every attractive quality we hope to find in others. Grace is a gift of the humble to the humiliated. Grace acknowledges the ugliness of sin by choosing to see beyond it...Grace is a gift of tender mercy when it makes the least sense."

WHAT'S THE POINT?: *Every major world religion except Christianity says your salvation depends solely on you. You must do more good than evil in your life. That's religion. God sent His sinless Son to be punished in your place. That's grace.*

> **If you earn it, then it's wages, not grace. And if you deserve it, then Jesus didn't have to die for your sins.**

PRAYER: *Loving, generous Lord, thank You for Your supreme gifts of grace. Lead me to dispense grace, as well as to receive it. Amen!*

INTERACT: How wonderful is the contrast between Romans 3:23 and 3:24?

_____
_____
_____
_____

Literally, 1 Peter 4:10 could mention God's grace in its *millions* of forms. Name a few benefits of God's grace in your life:

_____
_____
_____
_____

Recount a situation where grace triumphed over judgment.

_____
_____
_____
_____

DAY 82

GOOD OLD CHURCH WORD: SALVATION

> Therefore, if anyone is in Christ, he is a new creation; the old has gone, the new has come!
> —2 Corinthians 5:17 (NIV)
>
> What this means is that those who become Christians become new persons. They are not the same anymore, for the old life is gone. A new life has begun!
> —2 Corinthians 5:17 (NLT)

Of all the good old church words, *salvation* may be the one you are least likely to hear outside of church. It's common inside the cloistered walls of a church, but seems to have virtually no meaning or use anywhere else.

The good old church word for what God does for you is *salvation*, which simply means God saves you from the final, destructive punishment that was decreed for your sins.

What an amazing thing this is. God declares that any sin will be punished by death—then He offers to die in your place. What a deal, one too splendid and sublime to reject!

If you accept the death of Jesus Christ in your place, the result is being saved from awful and certain eternal death, the fair punishment for your sins. This salvation assures you of eternal life but also brings about great blessings now.

When we understand God's free offer of salvation, our response might be, "This is too good to be true!"

Too good to be true, yes...except, it IS true!

WHAT'S THE POINT?: *'Salvation' may be a good old church word, but it blesses every aspect of life, even outside church walls.*

PRAYER: *Thank You, dear God, for salvation, the preeminent gift of grace. Please save me and show me how I can reach out to others with this grand offer. Amen!*

> "Jesus is not one of many ways to approach God, nor is He the best of several ways; He is the only way."
> —A. W. Tozer

INTERACT: The context of 2 Corinthians 5:17 is "reconciliation." How is your reconciliation with God going?

_____
_____
_____
_____

I have experienced many blessings of salvation in my "pre–heaven" life. A few are:

_____
_____
_____
_____

Many object to the idea explained by A.W. Tozer above. Is Christianity unfairly restrictive?

_____
_____
_____
_____

What single product is desperately needed by every person on Earth and promises unequaled benefits?

_____
_____
_____
_____

DAY 83
WHAT'S WITH THIS *SANCTIFIED* BUSINESS?

> For them I [Jesus] sanctify myself, that they too may be truly sanctified.
> —John 17:19
>
> "Now I commit you to God and to the word of his grace, which can build you up and give you an inheritance among all those who are sanctified.
> —Acts 20:32
>
> It is God's will that you should be sanctified…
> —1 Thessalonians 4:3a

Our spiritual growth and development (what we have called follow-through) do not end with the acceptance of salvation. Accepting God's grace–gift of salvation is not just "eternal fire insurance;" it is accepting a whole new life.

The misery and sorrow that sin brings in this life do not have to continue. We can keep on growing, becoming more and more like Jesus. That's where this good old church word, *sanctification*, comes into play. It literally means, "To be set apart by God for some special use—a divine purpose!"

The origin of the sanctification idea arose in the Old Testament temple. The "operations manager" would order replacement pottery. Some were used for ordinary purposes, like waste holders and bins for cleaning supplies. But the best pots and jugs were set apart to be used for storing the special holy oil and the incense and other things used in the worship of God. They were *sanctified*.

For what special, specific purpose is God setting you apart? You may not know right now. God wants more than just weak tea for you. He wants you to experience a rich, delicious, abundant life.

God wants to give each of us a special purpose for living, here-and-now; plus, rest assured that God will bless you in the next life. *Sanctification* might not be heard much outside the church, but it plays a vital role in your life quality. And it's God's will for every Jesus follower. It's the essence of follow-through.

WHAT'S THE POINT?: *God has a special purpose for each believer. He wants to set you apart, to sanctify you, for His special purpose.*

> **God loves us just the way we are—but He loves us too much to leave us just the way we are!**

PRAYER: *Holy Spirit, I sense a deep need to be set apart for Your use. Please show me what You have in mind, and guide me toward that goal. Amen!*

INTERACT: What is "the word of God's grace" (Acts 20:32)?

_____
_____
_____
_____

I suspect God may be setting me apart (sanctifying me) for this special use:

_____
_____
_____
_____

Even if my spiritual growth is "two steps forward, one step back," it means I'm making progress. Here's how I'm more like Jesus today than I was one (day, week, month, or year) ago:

_____
_____
_____
_____

DAY 84

FOLLOW THROUGH TO HEAVEN

> **As soon as Jesus was baptized, he went up out of the water. At that moment heaven was opened, and he saw the Spirit of God descending like a dove and alighting on him. [17] And a voice from heaven said, "This is my Son, whom I love; with him I am well pleased."**
> **—Matthew 3:16–17**

Follow through is what happens *after* you hit the golf ball. It shows what you did *before* you hit the golf ball, which directly determines hook, slice or down the middle. In everyone's life, follow through and answer the inquiry, "What happens after I die?"

In recent years there has been a phenomenon sometimes called near–death–experience (NDE). Ostensibly, someone dies, then is transported into a long tunnel with intense light at the other end, all while feeling very peaceful. Many interpret this as a temporary trip to heaven before the individual reawakens in their earthly life. Some believe in the experience without reservation. Others are more skeptical. But while mystery shrouds the phenomenon, there are things we can know about heaven.

Every person who has trusted Jesus Christ as Savior in this life will spend eternity in heaven. It was created as the reward for everyone who trusts in Jesus Christ and begins to practice a life of love for Him. We have the promises of God regarding this.

Heaven is not just playing the harp. We might get tired of that eventually. It's not just sitting around on a cloud, looking down on everyone else. Heaven is a place of joy and happiness so superbly exquisite that we cannot even imagine it or find words for it until we have been there.

"Joy is the serious business of Heaven," said C.S. Lewis. So, be serious about going there. But hold the phone on exactly what heaven is like. We don't know far more things than we do know. You can trust Jesus to design and build it to your satisfaction. After all, Being Like Jesus means living by faith.

WHAT'S THE POINT?: *Heaven, a place out of this world wonderful, is the final result of living with godly follow–through. Take as many with you as possible.*

> **"The way you store up treasure in Heaven is by investing in getting other people there."**
> —Rick Warren

PRAYER: *Lord of heaven and Earth, I'm looking forward to heaven. I need your guidance to live with follow through. Amen!*

INTERACT: Why do you suppose the Holy Spirit appeared as a dove while alighting on Jesus (Matthew 3:16)?

_____
_____
_____
_____

Dissect the C.S. Lewis statement, "Joy is the serious business of Heaven."

_____
_____
_____
_____

I am accumulating heavenly treasure these days in this way:

FOLLOW THROUGH

DAY 85
HELL OF A PLACE

> "These people are springs without water and mists driven by a storm. Blackest darkness is reserved for them. [18]For they mouth empty, boastful words and, by appealing to the lustful desires of the flesh, they entice people who are just escaping from those who live in error. [19]They promise them freedom, while they themselves are slaves of depravity—for 'people are slaves to whatever has mastered them.'"
> —Jude vv. 17–19

Any discussion about what happens after we die is incomplete if we only think of heaven. Though its existence is disputed by many, and hated by many others, the Bible clearly presents hell as a real place to be avoided, whatever the cost.

Every preacher would like to declare hell a myth, but we cannot. Hell is presented in Scripture as such an appalling place, even those who believe in it don't want it to be true. There will be anguish, torment, suffering—choose any horrible description you want—for all who end up in hell. If believers got the tiniest taste of hell, we would work 24/7/365 to keep our friends and family, even our enemies, from going there.

If you refuse to trust Jesus Christ as your Savior (or you do not get around to it, or doubt it, or cannot make up your mind), your eternal destination will be a place as bad and agonizing and horrible as heaven is lovely and peaceful and delightful. Hell is heaven's opposite in every way. The very worst thing will be the absence of any God influence.

The Bible says God created this terrible place as the final punishment for Lucifer and those fallen angels who joined his mutiny. God's original plan did not include mankind as occupants of this dreadful place. But when the original couple joined the rebellion against God, hell was expanded as the place of punishment for obstinate human rebels as well. You can choose hell, too, by rejecting God's gracious offer of salvation. But why ever would you? God's love will carry the day.

WHAT'S THE POINT?: *We ignore or reject the Bible's teaching on hell at our peril. It's an awful subject, maybe the worst ever. The good news is, no one has to go there. Jesus died so you never have to experience hell.*

> "Hell is the highest reward that the devil can offer you for being his servant."
> —Billy Sunday

PRAYER: *Thank You, Lord Jesus, for taking my punishment and helping me escape eternal torment. I claim your great offer of heaven instead. Amen!*

INTERACT: Elaborate on "people are slaves to whatever has mastered them" (Jude v. 19):

_____
_____
_____
_____

I have known people who fit Jude's description in today's Bible reading. I have learned this about life from them:

_____
_____
_____
_____

"Mutiny On the Bounty" is the story of trading the joy of heaven for the devil's highest reward, hell. Why would anyone do that?

_____

_____

_____

_____

DAY 86

COSMIC COMBAT

> Jesus turned and said to Peter, "Get behind me, Satan! You are a stumbling block to me; you do not have in mind the concerns of God, but merely human concerns."
> —Matthew 16:23
>
> Submit yourselves, then, to God. Resist the devil, and he will flee from you.
> —James 4:7

In today's Scripture, Peter chides Jesus when He reveals He will die at the hands of His enemies. "Lord, this will never happen to You."

In response, Jesus does not say, "Peter, bite your tongue," as I might. He references "Satan!" The devil was using Peter for his own evil purposes. Peter was being motivated by "merely human concerns;" his worldview was not Jesus's life outlook. Been there, done that!

The most effective battle plan is to resist the devil, as James wrote. I picture Satan pushing on your heart's door. He knows you cannot hold it closed against him by yourself. But if the door does not open, he realizes that Jesus Christ is holding the door with you on the other side. So, he runs away in fear. That's the power of resisting the devil with Jesus's divine help.

This is a cosmic conflict, older even than Adam and Eve. The enemy of your soul is out there, and savvy Christians will prepare for the war Satan is waging against the human soul.

Spiritual combat is bad news, but take heart. There is good news too. Jesus fights alongside His people in this life–and–death struggle against evil in the world. "In this world you will have trouble. But take heart! I have overcome the world" (John 16:33b). Satan's doom is already announced, so from the get–go he is fighting a losing battle. If your goal is to be like Jesus, you will consistently read and study God's Word, develop a regular prayer life, join a community of believers that you can serve and look for divine appointments to speak God's love and power to those around you, even enemies of your soul.

WHAT'S THE POINT?: *To be breathing is to struggle with conflict. To be like Jesus is to enjoy His support in the midst of battle. Resist Satan and he will flee (James 4:7).*

> **"Every time you defeat a temptation, you become more like Jesus!"**
> —Rick Warren

PRAYER: *Blessed Savior, please build my spiritual fighting skills so I can avoid the destruction the devil lusts for me. Amen!*

INTERACT: How does Matthew 16:23 contrast the biblical and secular worldviews?

_____
_____
_____

Why is submitting to God so difficult (James 4:7)?

_____
_____
_____

I have used these tactics to resist the devil:

_____
_____
_____

Grade yourself on ☐ reading God's Word; ☐ developing a consistent prayer life; or ☐ speaking God's love to others:

0	1	2	3	4	5	6	7	8	9	10
Failing miserably					Sometimes faithful					Doing great

DAY 87

PARDONED FROM DEATH ROW

> "Everyone who calls on the name of the Lord will be saved."
> —Romans 10:13

The invitation to become more like Jesus is for three kinds of people. First, those who have never made spiritual preparations for life after death. The greatest need in life is to trust Jesus Christ as Savior.

Second, if you have trusted Jesus to save you but have never gone beyond baby steps of faith, what are you waiting for? Wouldn't you worry about your human baby not growing? Christians are either progressing or regressing. Which are you?

Third, the world needs "little Jesuses" who've trusted the Savior, have begun to resemble Jesus and who want to help others discover this wonderful life.

Want to explain to someone why and how to begin this rewarding journey? Take a little journey down the "Romans Road":

1. Every person has sinned and become separated from God (Romans 3:23).
2. God has declared that the just punishment for all sin is death (Romans 6:23).
3. Jesus Christ took your death penalty, bore the punishment for your sin, in your place. He has never sinned, but bore God's anger against sin so you can have an intimate relationship with Him. Forgiveness is available (Romans 5:8).
4. Forgiveness of sins is not automatic. You cannot depend on someone else's faith to make you right with God. God has no grandchildren. You must personally accept this wonderful, free gift of grace from God (Romans 10:9–13).

WHAT'S THE POINT?: *Being Like Jesus will profit everyone, from skeptic to firm believer. God has made it so easy to begin the life journey of faith.*

> "Saving us is the greatest and most concrete demonstration of God's love, the definitive display of His grace throughout time and eternity."
> —David Jeremiah

PRAYER: *Blessed Jesus, please guide me to become more like You, and to invite my family, friends, strangers and even enemies to trust You. Amen!*

INTERACT: What is the significance of "the name of the Lord" in today's verse?

_____
_____
_____
_____

Which of these three kinds of people in today's essay are you?

_____
_____
_____
_____

Odd as it may seem, some people find the easy path to God's forgiveness a hindrance to faith. "Just believe? It should be more difficult." Here's what I would say to that person:

_____
_____
_____
_____

- When it comes to sharing Jesus with others:

0	1	2	3	4	5	6	7	8	9	10
I just don't					It's hard, but I'm trying				One of my greatest joys	

8
THIS MEANS WAR

(Days 88–100)

To expand the impact of Chapter Eight, go to www.YouTube.com and enjoy "We Trust In The Name Of The Lord Our God" by Steven Green

DAY 88

WAR AND PEACE

> "Therefore, put on the full armor of God, so that when the day of evil comes, you may be able to stand your ground, and after you have done everything, to stand."
> —Ephesians 6:13

Civil War general Ulysses S. Grant is one of history's more interesting characters. He was not a great success at most things he tried. He graduated in the bottom half of his class at West Point. He spent a year before the Civil War working in his father's leather goods store. He showed little aptitude and was certainly an underachiever, considering his exalted education at the United States Military Academy.

His genius at making war became known only when he quickly rose through the ranks in the Northern Army during the Civil War, to Brigadier General. When President Lincoln could not find a competent general to lead the war effort, he turned to Grant, who was making a name for himself with brilliant military leadership. He validated Lincoln's confidence in him by turning the direction of the war and eventually reuniting all the states together.

In February, 1862, General Grant's army was besieging Fort Donelson, Tennessee. The Confederate commander sent a message, suggesting a cease–fire. Grant replied, "No terms except an unconditional and immediate surrender can be accepted." This message became famous, and Ulysses S. Grant became known as Unconditional Surrender (U.S.) Grant.

Shortly before launching his attack, a deserter from the Confederate army inside Fort Donelson turned up in Grant's camp. The general learned that the troops within the fort had received six days' rations, so he decided to attack immediately. "Gentlemen," he said, "troops do not have six days' rations served out to them in a fort if they mean to stay there. These men mean to retreat, not fight. We will attack at once." The enemy was quickly routed.

By early 1865, Grant's leadership had brought the Union Army to the point of total victory. He met Confederate General Robert E. Lee at the Appomattox, Virginia, courthouse. The surrender was signed, ending the war. Grant became President in 1868.

> "Whoever God loves, satan hates; whoever God blesses, satan tries to curse... [God's] children are the apples of His eye."
> —Theresa Pecku-Laryea, Hannah's Song

WHAT'S THE POINT?: *Like U.S. Grant, skill at warfare is vital for Jesus followers. No one wants war, but spiritual combat is unavoidable. It's Satan's nature to attack, and you must defend yourself or be destroyed.*

PRAYER: *Father God, I need Your close support to survive the devil's attacks. Help me thrive, not just survive the warfare, and win victory in my spiritual life. Amen!*

INTERACT: In matters of spiritual "war and peace," I stand my ground by doing this:

___

___

___

___

When was a specific time that, when the smoke of spiritual warfare cleared, you were still standing? What does that do for your confidence?

___

___

___

___

The battle–tested strategies of spiritual warfare I have found most effective are:

___

___

___

___

I hate spiritual battles, but I hate the result of losing even more. ❐ Yes ❐ No

DAY 89

ENDLESS WAR, CERTAIN VICTORY

> "Though we live in the world, we do not wage war as the world does."
> —2 Corinthians 10:3

The people who start wars are almost never on the front lines when the bullets fly. If war is glorious to anyone, it's only those who are not being shot at.

Out of six thousand years of recorded history, historians have identified only two hundred fifty-five years that had no reports of war somewhere in the world. War is a common experience of mankind. It is going on somewhere, virtually every moment of our past. According to the above statistic, only four percent of the world's history does not include a physical war someplace. At least ninety-six percent of the time, war has raged somewhere on planet Earth.

This sad reality of "constant war" applies in the spiritual realm too. Satan and his demons are constantly on the attack. If it's not you, it's your family members, church family, friends or neighbors. It makes good sense to know about this because whether you are a believer in Jesus Christ or not, Satan is out to destroy you. Jesus Christ, the Savior, is your only hope.

The Bible is packed full of warnings about the dangers Satan represents. It also has instructions about how to survive the universal blight of spiritual attack. Being Like Jesus means you will take spiritual combat seriously. Your eternal destiny depends on it.

WHAT'S THE POINT?: *We can't escape the cosmic warfare between God and the devil, but we can survive and thrive by serving our eternal Commander in Chief, Jesus Christ.*

PRAYER: *Perfect Lord Jesus, please equip me for the spiritual conflict ahead. You were victorious even over death. Guide me to triumph. Amen!*

INTERACT: Today's verse commands the intersection of the physical and spiritual worlds. Why is it difficult to orient yourself to the spiritual over the physical aspect of life?

> **There is good news on the war front: Many are fearful of the future, but the God Who knows the future will hold your hand.**

_____

_____

_____

_____

Some commanders agonize over harm to their soldiers. Others seem not to care. How can we account for this?

_____

_____

_____

If you hide your head in the sand about spiritual warfare, will it pass you by? Explain your answer:

_____

_____

_____

_____

Jesus experienced many conflicts with His attackers. Research the subject. What can we learn from Him?

_____

_____

_____

_____

DAY 90

THIS IS THE ARMY, MR. JONES*

> "You [Lucifer] said in your heart, 'I will ascend to the heavens; I will raise my throne above the stars of God; I will sit enthroned on the mount of assembly, on the utmost heights of Mount Zaphon.[a] 14I will ascend above the tops of the clouds; I will make myself like the Most High.' 15But you are brought down to the realm of the dead, to the depths of the pit."
> —Isaiah 14:13–15

[a] Or *of the north*; Zaphon was the sacred mountain of the Canaanite religions.

Every war has two or more armies. World War II had at least fifty countries engaged in hostilities and more than one hundred million combatants. That's a lot.

Spiritual warfare has two main armies involved, God's armed forces and the devil's opposing army. The commander of Satan's army is the deceiver, "angel of light," roaring lion, accuser of the saints. One–third of all God's angels defected when Lucifer rebelled. They make up his axis of evil, that quasi–military power that formulates Satan's strategy and carries out his tactical war on God's people.

The devil has two goals. The first is to undermine the rule and authority of God on Earth. Lucifer's pride drove him to take up the challenge of usurping God's supremacy, displacing Him throughout creation. His second objective is to destroy God's favored creation, humankind—you and me!

Demons are fallen angels loyal to Satan who were cast out of heaven with him. They do his wicked bidding, carrying out his plans, spreading terror and destruction wherever they go.

Humans also make up a sizable force within this evil army. Many are sworn to fight against the same things he wants to destroy. They may not even be aware of it, but their own personal wars against God and His people are really the devil's war being fought by human proxies under his clandestine control.

The Christians' hope comes from our Commander in Chief. His victory was earned at Calvary and in the empty tomb on Resurrection Sunday. The great news? He is risen, just as He said!

> "Because of His resurrection, we can have peace during even the most troubling of times. We know He is in control of all that happens in the world."
> —Paul Chappell

WHAT'S THE POINT?: *The great cosmic war between good and evil rages on. But God, through Jesus Christ, has already won the victory. We are safe under the banner of the King of kings.*

PRAYER: *Blessed Lord Jesus, guide and guard me in times of spiritual conflict. Use me as You wish, to bless others in their times of warfare too. Amen!*

INTERACT: What do you make of the pride oozing from Lucifer in today's Scripture reading? Did he really think he could supplant God?

_____
_____
_____

_____

Here's how pivotal Jesus's resurrection is to the Christian Faith (1 Corinthians 15:12–19):

_____
_____
_____

_____

*"This Is the Army Mr. Jones" by Irving Berlin

DAY 91
UNCLE SAM WANTS YOU!

> "Join with me [Paul] in suffering, like a good soldier of Christ Jesus. ⁴No one serving as a soldier gets entangled in civilian affairs, but rather tries to please his commanding officer."
> —2 Timothy 2:3–4

The devil's combat array is impressive. But it would be a grave error to think it is an even match against the Army of the Lord, with Jesus as commander in chief. This fighting force has God the Father, Son and Holy Spirit standing shoulder to shoulder against the enemy. That should encourage you. This powerful army includes God, but also angels and godly people who have enlisted, to round out its ranks. The Holy Spirit indwells and empowers each warrior to fight courageously and effectively against Satan's horde.

You can recruit the help of all God's Army in your own spiritual battles. Those forces include the faithful angels, created beings who have declared undying loyalty and devotion to Christ. Angels have become adorable figurines, the darlings of the collectibles industry. Amazon® can get you pretty much anything you might want, especially if you want porcelain.

Angels are more powerful than humans, but are not God. In reality, they are divine beings, sent with a commission straight from God to do His will—including warfare. Someone has suggested that angels make up God's air force.

Last on the list of God's spiritual war resources are His people, the weakest, yet the pivotal soldiers in the war to rescue humankind from Satan's devastation. Alone you have no chance against the spiritual forces of wickedness. As Jesus said, "Apart from Me, you can do nothing."

For some reason, God has chosen to do battle against sin and evil through Jesus's followers. If you approach the battle simply as an agent through whom God fights, you will succeed. If you think you're tough stuff, look out!

Bob Sorge in *Glory: When Heaven Invades Earth,* explains, "The nature of the enemy's warfare in your life is to cause you to become discouraged and to cast away your confidence...The enemy wants to numb you into a 'coping' kind of Christianity that has given up hope of seeing Jesus's resurrection power."

> **Commander in chief Jesus recruits soldiers for His army. But there is no such thing as a draft. Only willing soldiers for Christ need enlist.**

WHAT'S THE POINT?: *God fights evil with His own divine power, His angels and His people, the only formula against evil guaranteed to succeed.*

PRAYER: *Dear Commander in Chief, I'm joining up to fight alongside the angels of God, to win great eternal victories on life's battlefield. Amen!*

INTERACT: Is Paul's attitude toward suffering for Jesus (2 Timothy 2:3) common in today's landscape? Why or why not?

_____
_____
_____

What is the double meaning in Paul's words about a commanding officer (2 Timothy 2:4)?

_____
_____
_____
_____

When suffering for Jesus threatens me, I plan to:

_____

_____

DAY 92

MIND GAMES

> The weapons we fight with are not the weapons of the world. On the contrary, they have divine power to demolish strongholds. [5]We demolish arguments and every pretension that sets itself up against the knowledge of God, and we take captive every thought to make it obedient to Christ.
> —2 Corinthians 10:4–5

The *catapult*, the *longbow* and the *rifle* all had one thing in common: they changed forever the face of warfare. Today, it's a full-time job just keeping track of advancing military technology. It can be terrifying to see the murderous technological capabilities of guns, armament, aviation, communications, intelligence gathering, etc., in today's Army, Navy, Air Force, NSA, CIA, and others. The good news for Jesus's followers is that physical weapons do not have any bearing on spiritual warfare. As the Bible says, the Christian's weapons are not physical.

Demolishing the devil's strongholds, arguments and pretensions is the objective of Christian combat. Today's Scripture reading is a how-to: take captive every thought to make it obedient to Christ. In other words, the battle is won or lost in the mind. Proverbs 23:7 (NASB) says, "As he thinks within himself, so he is." And Jesus said that out of the abundance of people's hearts come the words they speak. Your thoughts and words shape the actions you take.

So, taking your thoughts captive and renewing your mind are indispensable if you hope to survive and thrive on the spiritual battlefield. Fill your life with God's Word, with praise and worship, with godly teaching and preaching, with like-minded friends. No room will remain for sinful, evil thinking. That's a good battle plan for success, satisfaction and living on purpose.

WHAT'S THE POINT?: *To overcome the wicked enemy of your soul, fill your mind with all that is true, noble, right, pure, lovely and admirable* (Philippians 4:8).

PRAYER: *Lord, please captivate my every thought so that I will be obedient to You. Amen!*

> "...when the blast of war blows in our ears, then imitate the action of the tiger; stiffen the sinews, summon up the blood, disguise fair nature with hard-favor'd rage."
> —William Shakespeare, *Henry V*

INTERACT: What strongholds are we called to demolish, according to Paul (2 Corinthians 10:4)?

_____
_____
_____

List examples of "pretensions that set themselves up against God" (10:5):

_____
_____
_____

I "take captive every thought" (v. 5) by doing this:

_____
_____
_____
_____

What "renewing your mind" activities are your favorites?

DAY 93
OPEN THE ARSENAL

> "Stand firm then, with the belt of truth buckled around your waist, with the breastplate of righteousness in place, ¹⁵and with your feet fitted with the readiness that comes from the gospel of peace. ¹⁶In addition to all this, take up the shield of faith, with which you can extinguish all the flaming arrows of the evil one. ¹⁷Take the helmet of salvation and the sword of the Spirit, which is the word of God."
> —Ephesians 6:14–17
>
> "Pray in the Spirit at all times and on every occasion. Stay alert and be persistent in your prayers for all believers everywhere."
> —Ephesians 6:18 (NLT)

The Bible explicitly describes seven spiritual weapons available for combat. The first weapon is the belt of *truth* (Ephesians v. 14), like the web gear in the pre–Iraq U.S. Army. It's a system of straps, snaps and loops that everything from the canteen to hand grenades clip onto. Similarly, the belt of truth holds all the spiritual soldier's other war tools in place, where you can easily access them.

Next is "the breastplate of *righteousness*," an early version of today's body armor. It protects those vital organs in the torso. This is God's provision for protecting your heart.

Third comes the footwear called "the *gospel* (literally, 'good news') of peace" (v. 15). With these combat boots (*hopefully your Mama wears them too*), the brave Christian can go out spreading the good news.

Then, the shield of *faith* (v. 16) protects you from the bullets, bombs and RPGs (rocket–propelled grenades) the evil enemy shoots at you.

Fifth, strap on the helmet of *salvation* (v. 17). It protects the all–

important head, the control center, from injury. Renewing your mind (Romans 12:2) and taking captive every thought (2 Corinthians 10:5) to make it obedient to Christ fit here.

Sixth, Paul says to pick up and use the sword of the Spirit—the *Word of God* (v. 17). This weapon has both defensive and offensive uses. With it, you can protect yourself in combat and also attack the enemy.

Truth, righteousness, good news, faith, salvation, God's Word. Six invaluable weapons that will help you win the battle.

I have saved the seventh weapon, *prayer* (v. 18), until now. Most lists do not even include it. What could be more useful in combat than prayer? Many battles have been lost because communications were cut off and vulnerable troops isolated. Without prayer, how can you cry out to God for His help? And without God's intervention, the battle is hopeless.

> **The sacred seven pieces of spiritual equipment are all you need to succeed in spiritual warfare.**

WHAT'S THE POINT?: *Use the full armor of God (Ephesians 6:10–18) to take no prisoners in the winner–take–all war of the ages.*

PRAYER: *Dear Lord, I desperately need Your help to win the victory and claim the eternal prize. Thank You for your support. Amen!*

INTERACT: Describe flaming arrows the devil uses on you:

_____

_____

_____

_____

Memorize Ephesians 6:14–18. Write it down to help cement it in your mind.

_____
_____
_____

Here is my report card for using God's armor in spiritual battle:

D−	D	D+	C−	C	C+	B−	B	B+	A−	A
Terminally deficient				Mixed results					Victoriously proficient	

DAY 94

TICKING OFF THE DEVIL

> "For if you live according to the flesh, you will die; but if by the Spirit you put to death the misdeeds of the body, you will live. ¹⁴For those who are led by the Spirit of God are the children of God. ¹⁵The Spirit you received does not make you slaves, so that you live in fear again; rather, the Spirit you received brought about your adoption to sonship. And by him we cry, "Abba,[Aramaic for "Daddy"] Father." ¹⁶The Spirit himself testifies with our spirit that we are God's children."
> —Romans 8:13–16

Some people picture the devil as a big, angry dog. Just let him sleep and you might be okay. Don't yank his chain, don't push his buttons. Let him snooze.

Nice try, except Satan never snoozes. It's not humanly possible to hide from, or avoid spiritual warfare. Buddha said life is suffering. Christians know life is a conflict against the devil.

Too many Christians think spiritual warfare is optional, or beyond their abilities, or just some wacky idea. The Bible is right—spiritual warfare is real. You can succeed if you remain grounded in Jesus.

Five spiritual weapons that Satan hates* are, first, *intercessory prayer*, seeking God's help for other people. It could be family, friends, neighbors, coworkers or even those with no one else to pray for them.

Next, *the name of Jesus* makes Satan grind his teeth in anguish. Use it often. If you were a soldier and you said, "The General sent me," you would receive complete cooperation. Think what the name of Jesus will get you.

Third, when you *praise God*, the devil hates it. One person defined praise as "Telling God how great He is, for your benefit." Think of praise and worship as Satan's Kryptonite.

Also, Satan hates the Christian's connection with *God the Holy Spirit*. When you are engaged in life–or–death warfare, He applies great power to the situation, protecting and guiding the Jesus follower.

Fifth, the devil detests what many call *"the Eucharist,"* which means, literally, the "good grace." This includes fellowshipping in Communion—sharing the Lord's Supper. When you share the good grace of God, the devil runs screaming from the room.

WHAT'S THE POINT?: *There is no escaping spiritual conflict. But victory is within every believer's grasp. Go ahead, give Satan what he hates most. Jesus has your back.*

Don't avoid antagonizing Satan. He already hates you. In fact, Satan is so full of hatred, he wants to destroy even those who serve him.

PRAYER: *Blessed Holy Spirit, please guide me as I launch into spiritual battle. Following your lead, we can tie the devil into knots. Amen!*

INTERACT: One time I was led by the Spirit that saved me trouble was:

_____
_____
_____
_____

Poking the "big dog" is not a game. Recount a time you and Jesus defeated the devil:

_____
_____
_____
_____

Here's how I will share the good grace of God with (use names):

_____

_____

_____

_____

* https://epicpew.com/5-spiritual-weapons/

DAY 95

LEARNING THE LANGUAGE

> Do not be anxious about anything, but in every situation, by prayer and petition, with thanksgiving, present your requests to God. ⁷And the peace of God, which transcends all understanding, will guard your hearts and your minds in Christ Jesus.
> —Philippians 4:6–7

Every summer the battlefields of Flanders, Belgium, burst forth with stunning red poppies. In 1918, the dead soldiers of France, Great Britain, Germany and the USA littered the ground like autumn leaves. Yet after World War–I, the fields returned to producing beauty, as they did before the carnage. Spiritual warfare has a battlefield too. It comprises two fields: the human mind and the human body.

Your spiritual problems begin when you listen to and consider the lies Satan tells. John 8:44 says that when the devil lies, he is speaking his native language. That means the language in which he is most fluent is *falsehood*. When Christian people believe the various and sundry lies he propagates, the wheels come off and victory goes off the tracks.

Like any good liar, the devil tells you what he thinks you want to hear. Even if it's untrue. Even—especially—if the end result will be pain, frustration, fear, and anger.

It's easy to blame Satan for life's mayhem. Sometimes, however, you need look no further than the mirror to find the perpetrator. Often the devil only needs to nudge you in the direction you're already leaning. Imploring God to help you lean toward Jesus is fundamental to spiritual victory.

The devil knows that his attacks against my mind are especially successful if I'm doing some mindless chore. When mowing the parsonage grass, I could look across the street and see the house of a man with whom I had experienced conflict. Before I finished mowing, the devil had me imagining hand grenades flying back and forth across the boulevard.

Relationships are priceless to God. The devil undermines our relationship with God and with others, first of all through the human mind. A personnel director I knew said that three-quarters of all job failures are people-related, not skills-related.

Turn to Jesus for wisdom in the mind's war against evil. God is eager to help you succeed.

> "So many people's problems are rooted in thinking patterns that actually produce the problems they experience in their lives."
> —Joyce Meyer, *Battlefield of the Mind*

WHAT'S THE POINT?: *The primary spiritual battlefield is the human mind. Fill your thoughts with the Bible, praise, and the beauty of God's creation. Crowd the devil out.*

PRAYER: *Father God, I'm lost without the godly thinking You promote to Jesus followers. Thank You for Your help. Amen!*

INTERACT: The word "guard" in Philippians 4:7 means *a fortress*. How does God's peace, even in wartime, shield and fortify you?

_____

_____

_____

_____

Artillery leaves destruction in its wake. What protection does the Christian have against such devastation?

_____

_____

_____

_____

These are activities I can do to fill my mind with all that is good (Philippians 4:8) and thus displace the devil:

_____
_____
_____
_____

I can identify these thinking patterns that lead me into spiritual trouble. I will use them in this way to win my battles against the evil one:

_____
_____
_____
_____

DAY 96

HE KEEPS GOOD RECORDS

> "Therefore, do not let sin reign in your mortal body so that you obey its evil desires. ¹³Do not offer any part of yourself to sin as an instrument of wickedness, but rather offer yourselves to God as those who have been brought from death to life; and offer every part of yourself to him as an instrument of righteousness."
> —Romans 6:12–13

It was one of the most important moments of their lives. But they did not know that then. The disciples followed Jesus to the Garden of Gethsemane, and when He went ahead of them to pray, they dozed off. They were supposed to keep watch with Him. Instead, their long, tiring day and the stress of the upper room (John 13–17) brought on the yawns, and they slept through a crucial moment in their relationship with Jesus. It happened three times on that Thursday night!

While the human mind is the main battlefield against the forces of evil, the human body is an adjacent combat zone. It has weaknesses that sometimes sabotage your spiritual well-being. Jesus told the Twelve, the spirit is willing, but the flesh is weak. And often Satan hits you there in order to destroy you.

Even though the devil attacks primarily in the human mind, he is determined enough to destroy us that he will also hit us in the physical arena when he can. This includes issues like illness, exhaustion, hunger or lack of proper rest, the lust to please the physical senses, and the preoccupation with material things and their ability to titillate.

Satan knows our weaknesses. He knows from long experience how to exploit them. My wise old mother used to say, "The devil doesn't know everything, but he keeps good records."

WHAT'S THE POINT?: *The vigilant Jesus follower will guard not only the mind, but also the body, through which Satan often attacks the Christian.*

> **The human mind is a huge battlefield. But Satan often enters the mind through the body and plants a seed of destruction.**

PRAYER: *Lord, keep me reminded that proper rest, nutrition, exercise and subjecting my body to Jesus, are all vital to spiritual success. Amen!*

INTERACT: What parts of yourself will you offer to God as "instruments of righteousness"?

___

Here is how Satan once used my physical self to defeat me:

___

Give one example of how the devil has kept good records on you.

___

Here is how I would explain to someone the "deliberate subjection of the body to Jesus":

___

DAY 97

CHURCHILL'S VEE

> "You, dear children, are from God and have overcome [the spirit of evil], because the one who is in you is greater than the one who is in the world."
> —1 John 4:4
>
> "...for everyone born of God overcomes the world. This is the victory that has overcome the world, even our faith. ⁵Who is it that overcomes the world? Only the one who believes that Jesus is the Son of God."
> —1 John 5:4–5

Every war has at least two armies, lots of weapons, battlefields where the conflict plays out, and strategies for defeating the enemy. But not every war has a clear winner and loser. Until Vietnam, the United States had never lost a war. Since then, many of our armed conflicts have been less than decisive. Such is not the case in spiritual battle. The Bible promises complete and total victory over Satan, far beyond any logical assurance we might have in earthly warfare.

History is replete with smaller, poorly-equipped armies defeating forces far greater. In the Hundred Years' War (1337 to 1453), England defeated France numerous times with smaller, more poorly equipped, sometimes diseased armies far from home.

Size plays no part in the war between good and evil. Pew Research has found that just 31.5 percent of the world's population claims membership in the Christian family. So, you can assume that the Army of the Lord must be smaller than her enemies' forces. Not that God and His might are overmatched by Satan. Exactly the opposite!

Someone has said that you, plus God, comprise a majority. The entire vast array of Satan's evil empire is lined up in battle formation against God's people. Yet the One who created the universe is far superior to all that the devil can throw at Him.

Winston Churchill flashed his "V" fingers and said, "Victory at all costs, victory in spite of all terror, victory however long and hard the road may be. For without victory, there is no survival."

WHAT'S THE POINT?: *Victory by the Kingdom of God is a sure thing. Though he fights with desperation, Satan's doom is certain. Choose sides, and choose carefully. Your eternal destiny awaits.*

> "Faith in God has not saved people from hardships and trials, but it has enabled them to bear tribulations courageously and to emerge victoriously."
> —Lee Roberson

PRAYER: *Lord God, I declare my loyalty to You. Give me my marching orders and Your mighty strength. Amen!*

INTERACT: Try to express the depth of meaning of the word "belief" in 1 John 5:5:

___

___

___

The Cathedrals gospel quartet sang a song, "I've Read the Back of the Book—and We Win!" How does that thought produce hope in your heart?

___

___

___

Describe the great celebration coming when Satan is finally overwhelmed:

_____
_____
_____
_____

DAY 98
FINALS WEEK

> Examine yourselves to see whether you are in the faith; test yourselves. Do you not realize that Christ Jesus is in you—unless, of course, you fail the test?
> —2 Corinthians 13:5

How could the week of final exams at any college bring on such a sudden cultural shift? How could students who have skipped classes, put off term papers, and partied at the expense of study make such a radical, though short-lived, change in their lifestyles?

The whole college town changes overnight. As final exams approach, students become uncharacteristically serious about schoolwork. They join study groups to review potential exam materials. They temporarily avoid beer and break out the coffee or Red Bull®. They burn the midnight oil. The administration gets in on it. The library, usually closed at midnight, is now open 24/7. The cafeteria has nutritious foods and stay-awake snacks. Local watering holes and pizza joints in town go all out to serve the suddenly studious population. In an academic sense, it could be Armageddon.

If you're thinking about becoming like Jesus, here is an exercise to consider. Before finals week arrives in your life (none of us knows when that will be), quiz yourself about your readiness. Are there notable spiritual victories in your past? Reminding yourself about them can give confidence and courage to press on.

Is your past littered with defeats, caving in to temptation, pain and frustration from the devil? Tell yourself, "Life can be better than this. And Jesus wants to help." Then find and practice the principles that move you toward Being Like Jesus.

What will you do about your future? Will you choose a victorious path in the great cosmic war of good versus evil in your life? Will you learn to think like Jesus? Will you continue with a mindset that includes the worldly, anti–God attitudes of Satan?

Final exams are coming. Don't put off preparation until it's too late. Like preparation for an exam, pulling a last-minute all-nighter is risky. God calls us to be like Jesus every day.

> "There are no secrets to success. It is the result of preparation, hard work and learning from failure."
> —Former U.S. Secretary of State Colin Powell

WHAT'S THE POINT?: *Being Like Jesus requires time as well as effort, concentration and devotion to Him. Turn life's distractions into occasions for worship, self-discipline, meditation and service.*

PRAYER: *Lord Jesus, guide my steps as I travel the path toward being like You. I know it's not just a sleepover, but a lifelong process. Amen!*

INTERACT: Explain the process of testing yourself, mentioned in today's Scripture, to see if you are in the faith:

_____
_____
_____
_____

Spiritual success does not depend solely on you. But it cannot start, nor move forward, without your permission. What do you need to do next?

_____
_____
_____
_____

Past successes—and failures—have helped me grow. Here is one example:

_____
_____
_____
_____

DAY 99

BODY PARTS

> "Each of you should use whatever gift you have received to serve others, as faithful stewards of God's grace in its various forms."
> —1 Peter 4:10 (NIV)
>
> "As each one has received a special gift, employ it in serving one another as good stewards of the multifaceted* grace of God."
> —1 Peter 4:10 (NASB)

In the 1980s, technology made it possible to display 16.8–million colors on computer monitors. The human eye couldn't distinguish the slight chromatic variations within close shades of a color. Yet scientifically they were different.

The vast number of colors within the spectrum illustrates the "various" or "multifaceted" grace of God. Such rainbow-hued grace demonstrates the myriad ways Jesus equips His followers to win on life's battlefield.

What can you do to succeed when spiritual combat is thrust upon you? Is there a strategy available to withstand the onslaught and turn the tide from hunted to hunter? Employ these strategies and see how Jesus comes to the rescue:

Read and study the Bible. Learn how Jesus thinks, and begin to pattern your mind, words and actions after Him. Do more than just learn *about* Him. Pattern every thought after Jesus's way of thinking.

Pray. Without systematic, intimate communication with God, spiritual victory hangs in the balance. But if you pray faithfully, you will find God at every twist and turn in your battles.

Prayer and Bible reading make up the dynamic duo of spiritual strategy in warfare. These two activities will give you a good start on successful Christian living. But it gets better.

Practice 'body life.' Such disciplines as worship, learning, and fellowship with other believers (all those "one another" passages**) describe 'body life.' The church is the Body of Christ, and every believer is a vital body part.

Serve others. Turn your gifts, strengths and interests into 16.8 million ways to help others in the mental–emotional, physical, spiritual, and social realms of life. The grace of God you are called to dispense in serving others is "variegated," "multifaceted," "prismatic," "rainbow colored."

You only get to do life once. With Jesus's help, figure out how you can maximize your success and satisfaction to accomplish the purpose of victory in spiritual warfare.

WHAT'S THE POINT?: *Spiritual disciplines make conflict with the devil much easier to survive and thrive. Don't hide your head in the sand, but seize the opportunities you have to lead the advance of Jesus's Kingdom.*

> "The temple of God is the holy people in Jesus Christ. The Body of Christ is the living temple of God and of the new humanity."
> —Dietrich Bonhoeffer, *The Cost of Discipleship*

PRAYER: *Spirit of Jesus, please guide me to make the most of my spiritual conflict, not only for my own benefit, but also to serve others for Jesus Christ. Amen!*

INTERACT: What special spiritual gift(s) has God given you?***

_____
_____
_____
_____

How are you using your gift(s) to bless His Kingdom?

_____
_____
_____
_____

Christians receive special dividends of God's grace (unearned, undeserved). We are also expected to dispense His grace. What might that involve?

_____
_____
_____
_____

What would maximum success, satisfaction and purpose look like in your unique set of circumstances?

_____
_____
_____
_____

Bible, prayer, body life, and service combine to produce spiritual vitality. Which one(s) do you need to enhance most?

_____
_____
_____
_____

* "Variegated" or rainbow–colored, distinct markings of many different colors

**for example, John 13:35; Romans 12:10 & 16, 15:7; Galatians 5:13; Ephesians 5:19 & 21; look for more. Hint: there are 64 in the NIV translation of the New Testament.

***Spiritual gifts passages include Romans 12:6–8; 1 Corinthians 12:1–11; Ephesians 4:11–13; Hebrews 2:4; 1 Peter 4:10

DAY 100

THE JUDAS COMPLEX

> "When Judas, who had betrayed him, saw that Jesus was condemned, he was seized with remorse and returned the thirty pieces of silver to the chief priests and the elders. ⁴'I have sinned,' he said, 'for I have betrayed innocent blood.' 'What is that to us?' they replied. 'That's your responsibility.' ⁵So Judas threw the money into the temple and left. Then he went away and hanged himself."
> —Matthew 27:3–5

Have you ever tried to get into the head of Judas Iscariot? Why did he betray Jesus? Was he jealous? Or maybe *greedy* is the word. Was he trying to manipulate the Son of God to lead a political rebellion against Rome? Can we be sure that we would not betray Jesus for some other, seemingly logical, reason?

"It is startling to think that Satan can actually come into the heart of a man in such close touch with Jesus as Judas was. And [worse]—he is cunningly trying to do it today. Yet he can get in only through a door opened from the inside. Every man controls the door of his own life. Satan can't get in without our [permission]" (S. D. Gordon).

Judas is a fascinating study about spiritual warfare. And a stark reminder that combat between good and evil is always with us, and is always to be taken seriously. Because "THIS MEANS WAR!"

WHAT'S THE POINT?: *Everyone wants a peaceful, conflict-free life. But both believers and unbelievers find struggle everywhere they turn. Being ready for it can be the difference between life and death.*

PRAYER: *Lord God, please equip me to succeed against evil. Give me the satisfaction that I have done the very best possible to represent You. Amen!*

INTERACT: My attitude toward the idea of spiritual warfare is:

- ☐ It is a little far-fetched.
- ☐ It makes me fearful, so I try to ignore it.
- ☐ I know it exists, and I'm trying my best to resist Satan.
- ☐ I regularly engage the enemy, and have victories (and scars) to show for it.

- In this realm of spiritual warfare, what should they write on my tombstone?

_____
_____
_____
_____

The area of my battle training that needs the most improvement is:
- ☐ Prayer
- ☐ Bible reading and study
- ☐ Body life with fellow-Christians
- ☐ Service to Christ and other people

If I had been in Judas's place, I would have:

_____
_____
_____
_____

EPILOGUE:

A LIFE OF ORDERED PRIORITIES

My wife Kathy is such a courageous soul. You cannot imagine the trials and tests she has gone through since September 16, 2021. She was rushed to the hospital shortly after midnight, and I did not see her again for ten days.

She lay in the Intensive Care Unit, fighting for her life against COVID–19. Her lungs were damaged, her strength was gone, and she had none of her cherished family to support her in person.

During those terrible days, and the Herculean struggle that followed, God met her at every turn. When she felt like she could not take another breath, God breathed His life into her. Some nights a praying nurse held her hand. One day, the top epidemiologist in the Midwest sat by her bed and shared his reliance on faith. And he asked her many questions about hers. Though she had hardly the breath to stay alive, God gave her miraculous strength not only to breathe, but to witness for almost an hour about God's blessings in her life.

Finally, on Sunday morning, September 26, 2021 I got to be with her, held her hand, and cared for the myriad little things she needed (a tissue, a refolding of the sheet, food to give her strength, and many tiny details that are unneeded today). It has been a privilege to take care of this extraordinary woman. She has been a treasure beyond diamonds in her loved ones' lives. We have blessings untold that she has showered upon us over these past fifty–plus years.

As I said in the Preface of this book, we are determined to leave each of our children a legacy of biblical wisdom, compassion, and faith. When we're gone, they will be fighting the good fight, as the Apostle Paul wrote in 2 Timothy 4:8. To everyone reading this book, please hold onto God with every fiber of your being. Your life can be a testimony of the godly heritage of good people who have touched you in unknown, immeasurable ways.

Please, order your priorities so that you will be an authentic Jesus follower. Take as many people with you into God's Kingdom as you can. Never believe the devil's lies, and always think, talk and act like Jesus.

When Kathy and I got home to western Washington state after our ordeal in Michigan, we read a daily devotional that resonated with our hearts. The Scripture verses are:

> **"And I am sure that God, who began a good work within you, will continue His work until it is finally finished on that day when Christ Jesus comes back again."**
> **—Philippians 1:6 (NLT)**

> **"Search me, O God, and know my heart; try me, and know my anxieties; and see if there is any wicked way in me, and lead me in the way everlasting."**
> **—Psalm 139:23–24 (NASB)**

Caution: if you make this your sincere prayer, God will likely shine the spotlight of the Holy Spirit on your life, illuminating things you need to change. It is never easy, but the rewards in terms of success, satisfaction and living on purpose will enrich your life as no gold, silver or bitcoin ever could. It is the outcome of *Being Like Jesus*.

Watch for the upcoming release of ***JOURNEYS FROM HERE TO ETERNITY*** by Dr. Curtis Alexander. Go to www.leadershipbooks.com

www.ingramcontent.com/pod-product-compliance
Lightning Source LLC
Chambersburg PA
CBHW070048080526
44586CB00013B/971